To Marilyn & Dick,

from D L Stewart...

and the woman who

promised to love me

and spend the rest of my [life?]...

THE MAN IN THE
BLUE FLANNEL PAJAMAS

The Least Bad of D. L. Stewart

D. L. Stewart

1977
Media Ventures, Inc.
Dayton, Ohio

LIBRARY OF CONGRESS CATALOGING IN PUBLICA-
TION DATA
Stewart, D. L., 1942—
    The man in the blue flannel pajamas
    Articles originally appeared in the Dayton Journal-
Herald.
    1. American wit and humor. I. Title
PN6162.S83   818'.5'407   77-18093
ISBN 0-89645-003-1

Credits: Cover—Pete Hironaka; back cover photo—Bill
Garlow; illustrations, pages 1, 30, 63, 89, 96, 122, 147,
176—Frank Pauer; photos, page 15—Walt Kleine (top,
lower left, lower right), Gordon Morioka (center), Bill
Garlow (lower center); photos, page 41—Walt Kleine
(top left, center left), Gordon Morioka (top right); photos,
page 138—Walt Kleine (top, second from right), United
Press International (lower left), Bill Garlow (lower, second from left), Ed Johnsey (lower right); photos, page
185—Walt Kleine (left), Al Wilson (top center, top right).

To Lynn, who promised to love, honor and make every day an adventure.

Contents

FOREWORD by Erma Bombeck

Chapter 1—THINGS THAT WOODWARD AND BERNSTEIN   1
       NEVER DID
    Upside Down in the Wild Blue Yonder
    The Night My Fangs Were Killing Me
    What, Me, Take Off My Clothes?
    Fastest Gun at the Dayton Mall
    Have You Ever Smoked a Sofa?
    He's Got the Time If You've Got the Jello
    How I Went Racing in My Blue Lace Dress
    The April Fool Pigeon and the Easter Beagle
    To Tell the Truth—or Lie for $50
    My Moment of Truth as a Phony Kisser
    The $116.67 Misunderstanding

Chapter 2—HOWDY DOODY, CHARLIE McCARTHY AND   30
       OTHER FUNNY PEOPLE
    Howdy You Like That, Never Heard of Him
    He's a Chimp, but Not a Chump
    A Funny Thing Happened on the Way to the Septic Tank
    Watch Out for Witches and Lance Collins
    It Takes a Dummy to Interview One
    King of the Cowboys Still Packs 'Em In
    Hi-yo, Aluminum . . . Away!
    Fastest Pizza Eater in the World
    Bill the Dill, Pickle Packing Promoter
    Tongue-Tied on the Left of Mr. Buckley
    Mr. Wunnerful Charms a Cynic
    But You Break Up When You See Him

Chapter 3—THE WOMAN WHO PROMISED TO LOVE,   63
       HONOR AND WASH MY BLUE FLANNEL PAJAMAS
    Baby 1, D.L. 0
    You Won't Have Any Trouble, She Said
    The Great Stork Race—In Real Life
    How I Still Missed the Big Game
    One Good Reason Not to Buy a Convertible

Those Old Piano Roll Blues
How Green My Valley, How High the Grass
Mower Trouble—And Where Is Mary Anne?
Don't Forget to Turn Off the Water
Mr. Build-It Strikes Again
Click, Click . . . Abort One Christmas Plan
A Little Yuletime Realism, Please
It's Not the Fall That Hurts So Bad
Fools Schuss In
The Rice Isn't All That Gets Fried

Chapter 4—WEIRD? WHADDYA MEAN WEIRD?   96
Children's Fare a Grimm Tale
Ms. Goose for the Seventies
Oh, Yummy! Poached Roach
There's a Worm in My Cookie
Count Hamstring's Revenge
Sorry, But a Fat Old Guy Isn't Quite Right
Yule Be Sorry You Read this
Porky Pig for the Defense of Larry
A Labor Day Fable
The Trouble with Horror Films
He Comes by It Honestly, Folks

Chapter 5—THE GAMES THAT GROWN MEN PLAY   122
Who's Crazy, Me or Those Sox Fans?
All the Answers on the World Series
In the Press Box with an All-Pro Tackle
The Inside Dope on the Super Bowl
Paul Brown: I Only Thought I Knew Him
Another Biggest Fight of the Century
Two Men Who Fight
And Then There Was Whammy
No One Gives a Toot Anymore
Soaring Saga of Soggy the Toad

Chapter 6—I SPENT A WEEK THERE ONE NIGHT   147
Well, Break My Bank!
On the Sidewalks of New York
And a Catfish at the Base of Her Spine

Not One Blessed Stomp or Whoop
Doing the Air Midwest Shuffle
It's a Saga, Plain(s) and Simple
Plains Just Goes Nuts over Jimmy
Let's Hear It for the Bull
A Hot Time in the Old Town
Disconnected by Mamacita Bell
The (Thr)ill of Deep Sea Fishing

Chapter 7—THE CLOWN'S DAY OFF   176
Hello, I'm Your Little Brother
Kim and Clifford and, Most of All, Tony
. . . For the World is Mine
An Everyday, Blind Belly Dancer
'There Is Music in Everything'
A Legend Who Still Takes It Off
Still a Message at America's Gateway
They Just Want to Make Friends
Why Don't They Let 'Rags' Be Happy?
Santa's Kid Stuff Still Works

Foreword

I have been asked to write a foreword for my dear friend, D. L. Stewart's book.

Even if I knew D. L. Stewart, the idea doesn't choke me up.

I mean, who reads forewords? In literary importance, they rank somewhere between a gin label and a steam iron warranty.

As any Ohioan worth his salt knows, the state has always been ridden with humorists. There were: James Thurber, Bob Hope, Paul Lynde, Jonathan Winters, Phyllis Diller, Tim Conway, Kaye Ballard, and the Kings of the one-liners, Wilbur and Orville Wright. Who could ever forget Orville's classic, "Have you seen my flotation cushion, Wilbur?" Wilbur: "No, Orville, is one missing?"

Through conscientious spraying, mass innoculations, and perseverance of the Sierra Club, they got rid of all of them — except one, D. L. Stewart.

I first met D. L. in a hotel lobby in Columbus, Ohio, where he was assigned to interview me throughout an entire day. I extended my hand and said, "Nice to meet you," and he turned to his cameraman and said, "If you thought THAT was funny, just hang around." He was to stand at my elbow for the next nine hours whining, "Is that it?"

FOREWORD

Long before that auspicious meeting, I had met D. L. Stewart through clippings—scores of them my sister enclosed with her letters from Dayton to Arizona. The columns were bright, funny, clever, and drove me, as an insecure humorist, right into the arms of my encounter leader.

I met Denny again while traveling through Dayton. He had just picked up his flight to Mexico. I tried to cheer him up by saying that my mother had actually gone to Mazatlan and become constipated, but humorists are basically depressing people.

As we talked, I wondered if the people of Dayton know how lucky they are to have a resident humor columnist of his caliber. A lot of cities say they do, but they lie. They're guys who hang around waiting for the phone to ring with handouts, write 40 inches on yogurt festivals, and at least once a month do a column on how tough it is to write a column.

Don't let his mouth which is overrun with footprints fool you. The guy is a real pro. When he was invited to the University of Dayton to lunch with conservative columnist Bill Buckley, the PR Rep said, "You're to Bill Buckley's left," and D. L. retorted, "Who isn't?"

Yep, you're gonna like this book. For all of you who have ever chuckled over World War II, found amusement in orthopedic shoes, and thought that leisure suits were here to stay, you'll laugh.

If enough of you laugh—who knows—D. L. may be able to go out and buy a first name.

—ERMA BOMBECK

1 Things That Woodward and Bernstein Never Did

Maybe the neatest call I ever got was from a gentleman who identified himself as the operator of a fishing lake.

"Have you ever ridden a catfish?" he asked.

"You mean recently?"

"Anytime."

"No."

"Well, here's what I have in mind. We have some catfish out here that go 40, 50 pounds. What I was thinking is that it would make a great column for you and some good advertising for me if you came out here and rode on one of them. How about it?"

"How am I supposed to ride a catfish? I mean, they don't have handles or anything."

"We'll put a saddle on it," the fish man said.

"Call me when you find a saddle that goes on a catfish."

I never heard from him again. Which is too bad, in a way. It might have made an interesting column at that. And I could have put it in this chapter. Right after the column about the lady who wanted me to jump into 600 gallons of Jello.

Upside Down in the Wild Blue Yonder

July 19, 1975

Looking back on it, it is obvious where I made my mistake. It is on the runway, when the pilot shouts to me:

"What kind of a ride would you like?"

Knowing what I know now, I realize that the smart answer would have been: "Oh, how about if we just taxi down to the end of the runway and then turn around and come back again?"

But, no, I had to play it cool. It's easy to play it cool when you've got all three wheels on the ground. So I give him my special sneer-in-the-face-of-danger grin and I say just as cool as you please:

"Whatever you want to do is fine with me."

And then he gives me a funny little smile and an A-OK sign with his fingers and five minutes later I am 2,500 feet over Moraine—upside down.

Looking back on it some more, it is obvious that saying "whatever you want to do is fine with me" isn't really the big mistake. The really big mistake is coming into the office earlier in the week and having somebody say, "How'd you like a free airplane ride?"

And I give my special scoff-in-the-face-of-fear chuckle and say, "Sure, why not?"

And then they tell me that the ride is in an old two-seat biplane, with no stewardesses and no movies and no complimentary soft drinks. And no top.

The idea of the whole business, I learn, is to draw attention to Dayton Air Fair 75, which is scheduled next weekend. The idea is that a bunch of news media people will take free airplane rides and that will help publicize the event and then a whole lot of folks will turn out next weekend at Cox Municipal Airport.

So I give my famous chortle-in-the-face-of-peril look and I go home to read a little Erica Jong and yesterday morning I show up at the Moraine Airpark.

The first person I run into there is Gil Whitney, the guy with the wooly worms. He is writing down the names of those who are going to fly. "So we can notify the next-of-kin," he says. I laugh at his little joke and make a mental note to watch Bob Breck from now on.

About a dozen news media people show up. Brad Clay of WAVI is there with a bottle of Dramamine. Don Postles is there. As we await our turns we talk, the conversation interrupted occasionally by a chuckle-in-the-face-of-terror.

Before I can think of a worthwhile emergency at home that I can rush to, it is my turn. With one last guffaw in the face of horror, I walk to the bright red biplane.

The pilot's name is Harold Johnson. He is the owner of the Moraine Airpark and a veteran of countless thousands of flights. He has, he says, never had any problems in the air. Unless you count the time he was sky-writing and the plane caught on fire. Or the time part of his propeller fell off and he had to land in the parking lot at the Ohio State Fair.

He directs me to the front seat of the Waco biplane, which was made in 1934 in Troy, Ohio. The front seat is reached by stepping onto the wing, turning around so that you face the rear of the plane, sticking your left leg into the seat, ducking your head so as not to make a hole in the top wing, bending over at the waist in a sort of reverse-limbo and doing a one and a half twist. In my fantasies, I had pictured myself looking like Tyrone Power hopping boldly into my WWI fighter. As it turned out, I looked like Kate Smith fighting her way into a '67 VW.

"It's a little greasy in here," I shout to Harold Johnson after I have pulled a majority of my limbs into the cockpit.

"Always is," he shouts back. "If there's no grease on the seats, that means the plane is out of oil. Then you've really got trouble."

I compliment myself on picking a plane that is well-oiled. I only wish that I was. I also reflect on how clever I was to wear my newest beige suit today.

Bumping over the grass to the runway, Harold Johnson shouts, "Are you sure you have your seat belt on tight?"

I double-check to make sure it is tight enough. My lower extremities have lost their circulation. That should be tight enough.

Then we are in the air, a smooth, effortless ascent. A gentle bank turns us around. We are cruising at 110 mph, the wind streaming past us. It is a snap. I look down. I-75 is below me on my right. The Great Miami River is below me on my left. The sky above is cloudy and gray. Suddenly, I-75 is no longer on my right. The sky below is cloudy and gray.

I remember Whitney's advice just before we went up. "If you want him to stop, just beat your hand on the cowl."

I want him to stop. The cowl, which used to be above me, is now below me. But I have no trouble locating it. It's my hand that I can't find.

As quickly as it went awry, the horizon returns to normal. I-75 is back on my right. The Great Miami River is back on my left. The sky is back on top where it was always meant to be.

Before I have a chance to beat on the cowl, we go into another stunt. We do a hammerhead turn. We do a loop. We do a barrel roll. Apparently Harold Johnson doesn't hear me beating the cowl with my hand.

The minutes fly by like hours, but finally we are back on the ground. I do my "Kate Smith fighting her way OUT of a '67 VW" imitation.

"That was fun," I say to Harold Johnson. I give him my snicker-in-the-face-of-nausea smile.

"Think you'd like to go up again sometime?" he asks.

"Sure," I say.

He thinks I'm kidding, but I am not. Someday I'm going to go back up there and get my stomach.

The Night My Fangs Were Killing Me

Oct. 30, 1976

First they can't find my nose and then they can only find one of my ears and before the night is over two of my claws have dropped off and my fangs are killing me.

I just never realized how tough it is to be a werewolf.

Of course, until Wednesday night, I had not had much experience as a werewolf. As far as I know.

My debut in the werewolf business came at the invitation of the Victory Theater Assn., which is staging a "Theater of Blood" this week. "Theater of Blood" is the Victory's answer to the haunted houses that spring up around here each Halloween.

"We've got about 100 volunteers, mostly high school students and a majority of the material has been donated and all the money we take in goes into the Victory fund," explains Dee Johnson, the woman who calls to invite me.

"Why don't you come down and we'll get you all made up like a werewolf and you can walk around and have a lot of fun."

"Do I get to say 'I vant to suck your blahd?' "

"That's vampires."

"You mean werewolves don't vant to suck blahd?"

"Nope."

"Then vat, er, what do they do?"

"Oh, they walk around growling and grunting and being nasty."

"You mean like Bob Kwesell?"

"You got it."

So on Wednesday, which is the opening night of "Theater of Blood," I walk over to the Victory. A sign on the front door says to go around to the stage door.

So I walk around to the stage door, which is pretty easy to find because about a half dozen teenagers are standing around it with their clothes torn to shreds and "blood" dripping from them.

I walk inside past the teenagers with the torn clothes and the dripping blood and the next thing I see is a bloody figure lying on the floor with its arm torn off and then a hunchback shuffles past me and a few steps further on I run into a girl with her eyeball falling out and resting on her cheek.

And I know right away that this place is going to be a million laughs.

Then I am introduced to Dave Kirby, the makeup man who will turn me into a werewolf.

"Hi," I say.

"Somebody stole your ears and nose," he snaps.

All the materials needed to turn me into a werewolf had been laid out carefully in the dressing room, Dave Kirby explains. But, somehow, the stuff got messed up and now he can't find the nose or the ears. The ears we can get along without. But a werewolf without a nose is like Cher without a navel.

While someone is dispatched to look for my nose and ears, Dave Kirby says we better get started, because it's going to take about 45 minutes to turn me into a werewolf.

First he puts on the wig. Then he takes a dish of something that looks like runny mayonnaise and smears it around on my face. He says it is liquid latex. All I know is that by the time he is finished smearing it on my face I feel like a potato salad.

Next comes the nose, which has finally turned up.

Fortunately, there is no trouble putting the werewolf nose over the real nose. It is fortunate, because otherwise I would never hear the end of it from the woman who promised to love, honor and never compare my nose to Danny Thomas's.

After the nose come the eyebrows and various other facial hairs. Normally the ears would go on next, but only one has been found. It is decided to skip the ears, rather than sending me out with only one and having people think I am J. Paul Getty's grandson.

After he paints the remaining areas of my face gray, Dave Kirby helps me on with the gloves. They are sort of like regular winter gloves, except that they have long claws at the end of each finger. And the fur is on the outside.

Lastly he hands me a set of plastic fangs. They are sharp. I know they are sharp, because as soon as I put them in they cut the inside of my mouth. They are not, in other words, the most comfortable teeth I have ever worn. I mean, they may be great for throats, but I wouldn't want to try them for corn on the cob.

After the teeth are in, I turn to look at myself in the mirror. I'm no expert, but it looks like a terrific werewolf face to me. As I stare at the hairy face in the mirror, I get an overwhelming urge to scratch behind my ear. With my hind foot.

But that is not the only overwhelming urge I feel. I mention the other overwhelming urge to Dave Kirby. He directs me to a little room at the end of the hall.

Inside the little room at the end of the hall I discover why men don't let their fingernails grow long and pointed. I can only assume that werewolves do not use little rooms at the end of halls. Or, if they do, they do it very carefully.

Then it is almost time for the "Theater of Blood" to open for business. Dee Johnson directs the monsters and ghouls to their places. My place is near the exit, in a tar-black maze. I point out to Dee Johnson that the effect of Dave Kirby's marvelous makeup work will be diminished somewhat by placing me in a tar-black maze where no one can see it.

She points out that this is why she is giving me a flashlight. When I hear people entering the maze, I am to flick the light on my face for an instant and then slink away into the darkness.

At 7:30 the doors are opened and all the volunteer monsters begin to do their stuff. Standing in the darkness, I hear terrible screams and wails. Hands and feet pound on the walls. Monsters shriek at each other from room to room. Which reminds me . . . I was supposed to call home at 7.

Finally I hear the first customers approaching the maze. I position myself in a dark corner, waiting for just the right moment. It sounds like a bunch of teenagers.

They are in the maze now. I flick on the flashlight. I lunge out of the corner. I emit a terrifying growl.

"Hey, man, have you seen Ralph?" the first kid in the line asks me. Kids raised on rock groups like "Alice Cooper" and "Kiss" are tough to scare.

I slink back into the darkness.

After awhile, I hear some more customers coming. Flick. Lunge. Growl.

"Oh, it's you," a woman says. "I read your column all the time. You look just like your picture."

She and her husband move off into the darkness.

"Who was that?" he asks.

"That's the guy who does the funny column in the paper," she says. "You know. Oh, what's his name? Uh . . . Bob Batz. That's it, Bob Batz."

I try again with the next group. Flick. Lunge. Growl.

"I thought you said you were going to call home at 7."

It's the woman who promised to love, honor and never nag if I occasionally forget to call home. She has brought with her the three oldest kids: Larry, Curly and Moe.

This was something I was looking forward to, having the kids see dad made up like a werewolf. What a treat for them.

The 12-year-old looks at me.

"Weird," she says. "Weird" is all she ever says.

The four-year-old looks at me. He is frightened at first, but the sound of my voice reassures him and soon he realizes that it is his father. I can tell he recognizes that it is his father by the way he kicks me in the shin.

The nine-year-old looks at me. He see my hairy face in the glare of the flashlight. He sees my wolfish nose. My pointed fangs. My sharpened claws. It is obvious that he is impressed.

"That's neat, dad," he exlaims. "Can I see your flashlight?"

What, Me, Take Off My Clothes?

July 29, 1975

I was, beyond a doubt, the best-dressed person at Paradise Gardens Sunday. Then again, I was the ONLY dressed person at Paradise Gardens Sunday.

Because Paradise Gardens is a nudist camp.

And, proving once again that no sacrifice is too great in the cause of journalism, I had dropped in Sunday to see . . . well, just to see.

Paradise Gardens is located on 35 wooded acres near the Cincinnati suburb of Groesbeck, about 60 miles from downtown Dayton. The final mile is a rocky, uphill, twisting road constructed by the same guys who did the Dorothy Lane crossing.

Pulling the remains of my car into a clearing at the end of

the rocks, I am greeted by Jim Wilson, the club manager. He is nattily attired in a pair of tattoos.

Jim Wilson is 34 years old. He and his wife, Sue, have been managing Paradise Gardens since it opened two years ago. They have been nudists for six years.

"It took him three years to talk me into it," Sue says as we sit at a picnic table with only one pair of bermuda shorts between us.

Paradise Gardens is one of three clubs in Ohio affiliated with the American Sunbathing Assn. The others are in Columbus and Medina. There are ASA clubs in 34 states. Alaska is not one of them.

About 60 families belong to Paradise Gardens, Jim says. Each family pays $112 a year for the privilege of walking around in their original factory equipment. Single men are not welcome, a bit of discrimination never mentioned by the women's libbers. Each applicant is screened for moral character.

"The class of people you meet here are generally a little bit above standard," claims Paradise Gardens owner George Stahley, who has just joined us at the picnic table. The ratio of persons to bermuda shorts is now 4 to 1.

According to the ASA literature, "as far as is known, not one child raised as a nudist has ever been arrested as a juvenile delinquent." It is a highly unprovable boast, of course. But for sure no one in a nudist camp has ever been arrested as an exhibitionist. Or as a pickpocket.

Lack of pockets is one of the inconveniences of nudism. There are others, I learn, as I begin to tour the camp grounds. A white-haired man named Larry offers me a beer. As I get the bottle out of the cooler in the back of his station wagon, he slides into the front seat to look for an opener. An instant later he leaps out. The car has been sitting in the sun for several hours.

Larry says he became exposed to nudism inadvertently eight or nine years ago when he bought a trailer from a friend. It was only after he had paid his money that he was told he would have to pick up the trailer at a nudist camp in Indiana.

"That was all right with me," he admits. "I wanted to see the naked women. Course, as you can see, 99 percent of them look better with their clothes on."

The embarrassment involved in nudism, most members agree, is short-lived.

"After the first 30 seconds, it's the most natural thing in the world," says Don, a tool and die maker from Cincinnati. "The initial steps were a hassle, but by the time we got to the pool it was all over."

"I carried in two lawn chairs the first time," says Don's wife, Nancy. "One in front and one in back."

"On the way over the first time I was tempted to say 'turn this car around and let's go home,' " admits Phyllis, who joined Paradise Gardens with her husband a month ago. "But after we got here I was undressed before he was. I guess a woman's just a natural nudist."

Jackie, who is 28 and made her debut a week and a half ago, isn't so sure.

"I feel like I've been shanghaied," she says. "The first time my husband mentioned it, I thought he was kidding."

Her husband is Doug, who says, "I've always felt this is the way it should be . . . just to be free with nature."

Doug is a teacher in Kentucky, one of the 16 states without ASA clubs.

"We're from the Bible belt," he notes. "I imagine if people found out I was a nudist, chances are I'd lose my job."

Doug is one of six teachers belonging to Paradise Gardens, according to Jim Wilson. The roster also includes a doctor, a farmer, a tow truck operator and, briefly, a woman who was on welfare.

A cross section of nudists, in other words, is no different than a cross section of any other group of campers. They swim, they play volleyball, they fish, they yell at their kids, they get sunburned. It's just that they get sunburned in more places.

Still, I don't know about this nudism business. I mean, if God intended for us to walk around naked, he would have made us that way.

Fastest Gun at the Dayton Mall

Dec. 8, 1975

Diary of a gunslinger:

SATURDAY, 10:30 a.m. — Alert and eager, I spring from my bunk. I have always been an early riser. Outside, the weather matches my mood. It is dark and mean, a perfect day for a showdown. The Last Annual Media Shootout, they are calling it.

10:35—I dress slowly, thinking of how it started; of how my reputation as a gun fighter grew from a column last month about the Dayton Blackhawks Fast Draw Club; of the challenge from Channel 2's Howard Ain. When you're a fast gun, there's always someone looking to build his reputation at your expense.

10:40—I think of Ain. He has hard, shifty eyes. He is good they say, real good. But today he will find I am better. This thing has been building up between us for too long. My trigger finger is itchy.

10:41—I scatch my trigger finger.

11:05—I am ready. It is time for the ride to town. "Is the gang ready to ride?" I ask my sidekick.

"Yeah," she says. "Soon as you put the stroller in the car. And don't forget the infant seat this time." She has hard, shifty eyes.

11:09—One of the gang says he's not sure he wants to go. He says he hates to miss *Return to the Planet of the Apes.*

"Mount up," I snarl. That's how Jesse James would have handled it.

11:45—We mosey into the Dayton Mall, where the shootout will take place. The Dayton Blackhawks are already here, to make sure it is a fair fight. I am glad to see them. The showdown wouldn't be the same without them. They have the guns.

11:48—A large crowd has gathered. Off in the distance I see Santa Claus. He has hard, shifty eyes. Ain has not shown up yet, but there are plenty of other mean-looking varmints around.

There is Bucky "The Kid" Albers in his authentic Mexican

sombrero and his authentic blue tennis shoes. There is Doc Creep, dressed, as usual, all in black. There is Sheryl Previll, with her long blonde hair falling over her crew-neck sweater. They don't make mean-looking varmints like they used to.

11:55—Ain swaggers into the mall. Outwardly he appears calm and confident, but I know what is happening inside him. You can always see the telltale signs: the slight shaking in his hands, the glassy look in his eyes. I have been there too many times not to be able to recognize them. He has a hangover.

"You ready?' he says.

Yep.

HIGH NOON—Before our showdown, there are some other scores to be settled. It will be done in the traditional way of the West: three shots each with wax bullets at the steel target seven feet away. Best total time wins. The wax bullets are not dangerous. Except to wax people.

12:02—Doc Creep and P.J. Bednarski are first. At the signal, they draw and fire. Creep nicks his target. P.J.'s gun fails to shoot. "Save the redwoods," he yells.

12:06—Skip Hapner guns down Albers.

12:11—Sheryl Previll and Connie Lockwood face off. In dazzling displays of trick shooting, they both plug the wall three times. It is a skillful exhibition, seeing as how those large targets were in their way.

12:16—Bob Kwesell is dispatched by Bob Batz, who wins a trophy for the day's best combined times.

12:20—Tom Beres draws first blood for the TV-2 gang when he beats Johnny Walker. Unfortunately, the blood is his own. He has cut his hand on his gun. A doctor is called for. Doc Creep arrives. Beres decides he'd just as soon bleed.

12:25—Steve Hall saves WAVI's honor by shooting down Judy Houck of Channel 7.

12:30—Now only the two of us are left. There is nowhere for Ain to hide. If he loses he has said, he will get out of town. If he wins, he also will get out of town. I figure the odds are in my favor.

12:35—We are side by side facing the targets. The signal is given and I slap leather. Bad move. I should have drawn my gun.

Incredibly, I miss the target. Obviously a faulty bullet. But Ain does no better.

12:38—We are set again. Signal. Draw. I am greased lightning as I plug the target with the fastest draw seen here on this day. Ain is not even close.

12:41—It is Ain's last chance. As one, we draw. As one, we fire. As one, we miss our targets by about a mile and a half.

12:42—Hopalong Howard Ain has become the latest notch on my gun. He will have to get out of town.

12:45—Victoriously, but with great modesty, I walk over to my sidekick. I am Wyatt Earp approaching the sheriff's daughter. Bat Masterson strolling over to the schoolmarm.

I look down at her. She looks up at me.

"Shucks," I say.

"Now that you're done fooling around, can we take the kids down to see Santa Claus?" she says.

Have You Ever Smoked a Sofa?

Mar. 26, 1976

Author's note: The following story is true. If questioned by the proper authorities, however, I will deny every word of it.

I was just sitting there. Honest. Minding my own business and sipping a Canadian Mist and Sprite, because that's just about all that was left at this party that I was at not long ago. Except for some tequila, which I wasn't about to try because you never know about those foreign drinks.

Anyway, I'm just sitting there drinking my drink and puffing my cigarette when this woman I had met earlier walks up to me and says:

"Do you smoke?"

Which seems like a pretty silly question to me, because at that very moment smoke is pouring out of my mouth and it seems obvious that either I smoke or my stomach is on fire.

So I point to the cigarette, which at that very moment is creating yellow stains on the fingers of my right hand.

But the woman says:

"No. I mean do you SMOKE?"

And suddenly I understand where she is coming from and where her head is at and all that kind of talk. She is asking me if I smoke marijuana.

So I tell her that the only thing I know about grass is that it takes four hours to cut every week and no matter what kind of stuff you put on it it's always filled with chickweed and dandelions.

And she says that a bunch of folks are going up to her hotel room to smoke a little and if I want to come along, I'm welcome.

The next thing I know I'm going up on the elevator with half a dozen other people whose names I can't really remember and whose faces I would never be able to pick out of a lineup.

As the elevator makes its ascent, all the stories I have ever heard about drugs skip through my head.

The way I have heard it, grass leads to LSD and LSD leads to cocaine and cocaine leads to heroin and pretty soon you're out on the street selling your body to support your habit.

Just as I am wondering what kind of price I would be able to get for my body, the elevator door opens and we are heading to the room where the stash is stashed.

Then we are in the room and somebody opens the glass patio door, the one that says, "Be sure this door is locked at all times." Meanwhile, somebody else is getting the stuff together and I take a look at it and I am surprised to see that it doesn't look like grass at all. It looks more like oregano.

For a moment I think that perhaps I have made a mistake and that I have been invited to a chicken cacciatore party.

But then some cigarette papers are produced and a guy sprinkles some of the grass onto one and rolls it up. And when he is finished it looks like a deformed Pall Mall.

Then he is lighting it and about half of it instantly disappears in a burst of flame. A few seconds later I begin to believe that that was the good half, because the part that remains is giving off an odor that makes me think of the time the sofa caught on fire.

With my first sniffs of burning grass comes the realization that I am really at my first pot party.

In the cockpit, behind the gun, with fangs, in blue lace,
and ready for Jello.

Right then I am seized by the fear that at any moment the
narcs will come bursting through the door with their special
dogs and they will haul us all away.

A lifetime of obeying the law, of always paying my parking
tickets and never crossing when the sign says "Don't Walk"
will be ruined.

But it is too late to back out now. The joint, having been
passed from hand to hand, from lip to lip, is being offered to me.

"Take a deep drag and hold it in," someone is saying. "But
try to draw a lot of air in with it."

So I draw on this thing that smells like a burning sofa,
wondering what it is going to do to me.

Will it make me feel warm and free and happy?

Or will it make me feel evil and depraved and miserable?

As I hold the smoke in my lungs, I feel neither of these things. As I hold the smoke in my lungs, I feel like I am smoking a sofa.

Soon another joint is lighted and it's starting to smell as if the whole living room is burning. I try one more drag on the new one, but it tastes no better than the other. What's worse, I don't feel high at all. Only foolish.

As far as I can tell, no one else in the room is getting high, either. Except, maybe, for the guy who is trying to convince everybody that ducks are an endangered species. I sit around for awhile, not smoking, just listening.

One woman is talking about spending the weekend on Dexedrine, Twinkies and Coke. Two guys are discussing the best way to make tea out of a certain mushroom that grows in cow dung. When they get to the part about how you can eat the mushrooms, fresh-picked, I decide to leave.

I'll probaby never smoke another joint. For sure I'll never eat another mushroom.

He's Got the Time If You've Got the Jello

Apr. 23, 1977

I suppose the highlight of the day was when Roz Young paid me a nickel to drop my pants.

Which almost made up for the two times I didn't get to jump into the Jello.

To understand about Roz Young and the Jello and me dropping my pants, you've got to be aware that out at the Salem Mall various charitable organizations have set up booths this weekend to raise money.

Among the groups is the Human Growth Foundation (HGF), which is digging into the causes and treatments of the growth problems that afflict 500,000 persons in the United States.

At its booth, HGF has constructed a large wading pool and filled it with 600 gallons of cherry Jello. For a $1 "donation," people are invited to walk, wade, waddle or wallow in it.

"If you'd like to come out and be the first one in, we'd be

glad to have you," says Beth Craycraft, who is coordinating the event.

Having already decided that what this newspaper sorely needs is a first-person story from a Jello-jumper, being the first one in has double appeal.

If I am the first one in, it will be yet another example of *The Journal Herald* keeping its readers a wallow ahead of the daily news. Besides, I figure they're probably not going to chlorinate that Jello.

My next move is to notify our photo department. On my way home I stop at a costume shop and rent a turn-of-the-century bathing suit, to liven up the picture.

"Did you get one that covers the upper half of your body?" asks the woman who promised to love, honor and keep a firm grip on my love handles.

"Yes."

"Good. That way, when you're lying in the pool, people will be able to tell which is you and which is the Jello."

When I arrive at the mall, the photographer is there, the pool is there and HGF Director of Development Mike Mitchell is there. But the Jello is not there.

"Where's the Jello?" I ask.

"It's on its way from Chicago," Mike Mitchell says.

Resisting my natural inclination to ask how one ships 600 gallons of Jello, I ask him what it was doing in Chicago in the first place.

"Coming from Minneapolis," he says. "It was supposed to be here last night, but it got delayed in Chicago. It should be here soon."

"Instead of waiting around for it, why don't you just go out and buy some at Kroger's?"

"It would take quite a few boxes."

"How many?"

"3,600."

Mike Mitchell assures me that the Jello will be here and suitable for wallowing by mid-afternoon. So I drive back to work, with the turn-of-the-century bathing suit under my clothes.

At work I encounter Roz Young. She is sitting at the desk

in her office, repairing split infinitives. I tell her about the Jello and show her the top of my turn-of-the-century bathing suit.

"Give me a nickel and I'll show you the bottoms," I joke.

"All I have is a dime," she says.

"You can look twice."

"Once should be plenty."

After I have pulled up my pants and made change, I leave Roz Young's office. It is time to go back to the mall.

When I get there, the Jello has arrived. But it is not in the pool. It is in a garbage can. The reason it is in a garbage can is that Mike Mitchell and Beth Craycraft could not find a sauce pan suitable for making 600 gallons of Jello.

I peek into the garbage can, the contents of which do not look anything like cherry Jello. For one thing, it does not have any fruit cocktail in it. Besides, it isn't even red.

"I don't know a whole lot about cooking, but isn't cherry Jello supposed to be red?" I ask Beth Craycraft, who is stirring the stuff with a canoe paddle.

"It will be," she says, "as soon as we put the coloring in."

"Oh. Do you have to put sugar in, too?"

"No sugar."

"Good. I'm on a diet."

After half an hour or so of stirring, it becomes obvious that the Jello is not going to be ready in time for me to be able to write about wallowing in it. So I explain to Mike Mitchell and Beth Craycraft about deadlines and press runs and screaming editors and then I head back to work, driving quickly.

But I'm too late. Roz has already taken her other nickel and gone home.

How I Went Racing in My Blue Lace Dress
May 17, 1977

Just so you don't get the wrong idea, I want to say right at the beginning that wearing a blue lace dress was not my idea. I would much rather have worn the plaid cotton frock.

But the plaid cotton frock just didn't work out. So I simply had no choice but to wear the blue lace dress for my appearance last week in the third annual Cpl. Klinger Drag Race at Wright State University.

The Cpl. Klinger Drag Race is sponsored by the Veterans Educational Organization (VEO), a Wright State group involved in the education of veterans. The race is named in honor of a character on the TV show *M*A*S*H* who spent the Korean War wearing dresses because he didn't have the courage to shoot himself in the foot.

In past years, the race was limited to students, but this year a celebrity division is added. Already entered, I am told, are Gil Whitney, Bill Nance and Patty Spitler.

So, when my invitation arrives, I quickly agree to participate, with barely a thought for what damage it might do to my reputation as a skilled journalist.

Finding a dress my size (40-long) is easier than I expected. A woman at work digs two of them out of her attic. She also supplies me with a sheer pink scarf, a pair of white nylon gloves and a little pink hat with an ostrich feather on it.

I take them home and try them on. The blue lace fits fine, but I am not convinced blue lace is really me. So I try on the other one, the plaid cotton frock. It is very wrinkled. But it matches my eyes.

"What do you think?" I ask the woman who promised to love, honor and tell me when my hem was crooked.

"I think we're getting separate bedrooms," she says.

"C'mon, be serious. I think if you iron this one it'll look stunning on me."

"Wait a minute, sugar. I listened to the wedding vows very carefully, and not once did anybody mention anything about me having to iron your dresses. If you want to wear that dress, you're going to have to wear it wrinkled."

"What? And have people think I'm strange? No thanks. I'll wear the blue lace."

On Friday, I pack the blue lace, the sheer pink scarf, the white nylon gloves, the little pink hat with the ostrich feather on it, a fashion coordinated black and orange purse and a necklace I have borrowed from the guy next door.

I drive to Wright State and find my way to a men's room in Allyn Hall. In the men's room I put on the dress, gloves and hat.

Just as I am tying the sheer pink scarf under my chin, a guy walks in. He is sort of hopping up and down. He looks at me. I smile at him. He backs out of the men's room, mumbling something I cannot quite catch. He is still hopping.

Feeling like a low-budget Milton Berle, I leave the men's room and walk to Founder's Quad, around which the race is to be run. I am not familiar with the WSU campus, but I know I am in the right place when I see a guy wearing a green mini-dress and panty hose talking with another guy who is wearing a blue and orange striped dress and bright red lipstick.

For a moment, I can not believe my eyes. I mean, bright red with a blue and orange dress?

The tacky guy's name is Gale Alley, and he is the president of VEO. I ask him where the other media folks are.

"You're the only one who showed up," he says. Which is an indication of my reliability. Not to mention my desperation for column material.

With no other media people on hand, it is decided to put me in the race with the college students. The race will be two laps around Founder's Quad, roughly a quarter of a mile.

The race starts. Dress flapping, necklace bouncing, I jump into the lead. Behind me, I can hear the half dozen other competitors.

The race continues. Arms pumping, legs slashing, I remain in the lead. Behind me, I can sense the half dozen other competitors.

The race goes on. Heart pounding, stomach churning, my chances of victory are not as good as they once were. Ahead of me, I can barely make out the half dozen other competitors. Shortly after that, I reach the first turn.

By the time I complete one lap, I know why it is called a drag race. My tongue is dragging. It is not alone.

The blue lace dress has gained about 30 pounds. The necklace keeps hitting me in the face. The purse hangs like an anvil from my wrist. I finish 50 yards before the race does. It is a miserable showing.

Next year, I vow, I will come back for the 4th annual Cpl. Klinger Drag Race. Next year, it will be a different story. Next year, I will wear the plaid cotton frock.

The April Fool Pigeon and the Easter Beagle

Apr. 2, 1977

I begin to suspect that yesterday is going to get out of control when I walk into the office and the lady who takes phone messages says there is a call for me concerning a pigeon.

Not being a statue, I have no particular feelings about pigeons one way or the other. But I have a rather full agenda today. I tell the phone message lady that.

"I'm up to my armpits in work and the last thing I'm gonna do is return some stupid call about some stupid pigeon. I got better things to do with my time than to worry about stupid birds."

"She sounded pretty," the phone message lady says.

"Gimme that number again."

The caller's name is Tricia. She works in the Grant-Deneau Tower. If I call her, she will tell me her story. I call her. She tells me her story.

There is a pigeon trapped in a vacant office in the building across the street from where she works, she says. So she called the building manager's office to tell them about it.

"When I told the girl in the building management office," Tricia says, "she just sort of went 'uh-huh,' like she thought it was probably an April Fool's Day joke.

"So a little later I called back and got another girl. But I don't really think she believed it, either.

"Anyway, I just thought you might be interested in hearing how hard it is to get people to believe you on April Fool's Day."

"Is this an April Fool's joke?" I ask.

"No," Tricia says, "it's true."

So I thank her for her call and hang up. Then I call the building where the alleged pigeon is trapped, just to double check. Double-checking won the Pulitzer for Woodward and Bernstein.

"Is this the place with the pigeon?"

"Yes it is," the lady says. "It's down on the ninth floor."

The pigeon building lady says she has no idea how long the bird has been there, or even how it got into the building. "Maybe it was born there," I suggest.

While she is laughing, it occurs to me that perhaps there

really is a column here. Maybe I should go over and let that bird out myself. Properly written, it might make a good piece. Maybe even a prize winner.

I picture the headline:

Pulitzer Prize to pigeon freer

I mention to the lady that I'd like to come over and emancipate the bird.

"Oh, I don't know," she says. "I'll have to get permission from the building manager. I'll call you back."

While I am waiting for the call that could make me a star, a delivery man comes into the office.

"You D. L. Stewart?"

"Maybe."

"Well, if you are, I have a package for you."

"Is it ticking?"

"Nope."

"I'm D.L. Stewart."

He hands me the package. Inside, there are a dozen pink roses. They are from a young lady in Huber Heights in commemoration of the second anniversary of my column.

I have never received flowers before. As far as I know, no man in our office has. But that doesn't bother me. What bothers me is the company rule that we are only allowed to accept those gifts we can eat in one day.

I am on my fifth rosebud when the pigeon building lady calls back. The pigeon has been released, she says. She apologizes for not being able to get permission for me to do it.

That's all right, I assure her. Going all the way to New York to pick up the Pulitzer is a hassle anyway. I hang up the phone.

A few minutes later, it rings again.

"Is this D.L. Stewart?"

"Yes."

"Mr. Stewart, do you believe in the Easter Beagle?"

"Doesn't everybody?"

"Oh good. He'll be at your office next Friday."

"Will he be ticking?"

"Of course not. He's visiting all the good little boys and girls. You have been a good boy, haven't you?"

"Well, my mother hasn't sent me to bed without my supper this week."

"Good. The Easter Beagle will be there."

"I'm looking forward to it."

I hang up. I've got to get out of this job.

The monotony is driving me crazy.

To Tell the Truth—or Lie for $50

July 12, 1977

NEW YORK—When I was even younger than I am now, my college roommate and I pooled our worldly wealth and we hitchhiked to New York City with the $20 burning holes in our pockets.

For two days we rode the subways and we wandered the outside lobbies of the United Nations building and we strolled past Lindy's and Sardi's and Radio City Music Hall.

Then someone told us some television shows had no admission charge, so we rushed right down to the Ed Sullivan Theater with visions of Jackie Gleason and George Gobel dancing in our heads.

What we got was *To Tell The Truth.*

I really don't remember much about the show. All that sticks in my mind is that the audience was instructed to applaud enthusiastically at the proper times . . . or else.

Nobody actually said "or else," of course, but you could tell that something bad would happen to you if you didn't applaud enthusiastically at the proper times.

So we applauded enthusiastically, my roommate and I.

For the first half of the show we applauded enthusiastically because we figured that if we didn't, an usher would come along and make us leave. After awhile we applauded enthusiastically because we figured that if we didn't, an usher would come along and make us stay.

That was 15 years ago. Ed Sullivan has gone to that really big show in the sky and Jackie Gleason is having face lifts in Florida and George Gobel is sitting around somewhere telling jokes to spooky ol' Alice.

And, in New York, they're still cranking out *To Tell The Truth*.

Although it is not a network show, *To Tell The Truth* is: taped each Wednesday in studio 8H at NBC.

So I go to Rockefeller Center, which is where NBC is, and a red-jacketed security guard issues me a pass which I am required to carry with me at all times so people will not confuse me with Tom Brokaw.

In Studio 8H, I introduce myself to Bruno Zirato, the show's executive producer.

"Why didn't you move this show out to Hollywood like all the others?" I ask him as we wait for the taping of show No. 3161 to begin.

"You get better contestants here," he explains. "To be an imposter on this show requires method lying and people in New York are better at it. Plus there's more variety here. New York is a metropolis. Hollywood is a film studio."

Then it is time for show No. 3161 to begin. Instead of sitting in the audience, I am allowed to sit in the control booth. In the control booth, people are not required to applaud. All they have to do is yell and scream and tear out their hair. It is a lot like a newspaper office.

The plot of show No. 3161 is whether the celebrity panel will be able to correctly identify Robin Cook, the author of a book called *Coma*.

The show proceeds. Suddenly the level of yelling, screaming and hair pulling intensifies. "What's that noise?" someone in the control room shrieks. "What the hell's that noise?"

That noise, it turns out, is contestant No. 3 playing nervously with his microphone. During a commercial the problem is taken care of. I am not exactly sure how. But I suspect No. 3's fingers are chopped off.

The show comes to a successful conclusion. The real Robin Cook stands up. The audience applauds enthusiastically.

"That was interesting," I say to Bruno Zirato. "Thanks for letting me sit in here."

"No problem," he says. "Say, why don't you come on the show sometime? You could be one of the imposters."

"Geez, thanks, but I don't think so. I really sweat when I get in front of a TV camera."

"Don't worry, there's nothing to it."

"Yeah, but, I'd probably make a bunch of mistakes."

"You'd have plenty of rehearsals."

"The thing is, newspapermen don't know how to lie."

"You'd get a minimum of 50 bucks."

"Here's my number."

NEXT: My name is, uh, er . . .

My Moment of Truth as a Phony Kisser

July 14, 1977

NEW YORK—The phone call that I have been dreading comes on a Thursday.

It is from Goodson-Todman Enterprises Ltd. Among Goodson-Todman's limited enterprises is *To Tell The Truth,* a nationally syndicated show which suggests that two out of three people you see on television are fakes.

In a moment of insanity while interviewing the show's executive producer, I had agreed to appear on the show as an imposter should the occasion ever arise.

The phone call on Thursday is to tell me that the occasion has arisen.

"When?" I ask the lady at the other end.

"Next Wednesday," she says.

"Who will I be impersonating?"

"His name is Joe Jeff. He teaches at a university in Washington."

"Oh. Well, I'd better do some research so I'll be well prepared. What does he teach?"

"Kissing."

"Oh."

I promise to be there on Wednesday and then I hang up. There is no escape now. In six days I will be taping a show that will be seen in more than 100 markets by 12 million viewers.

My little heart is going pitty-pat.

I start rehearsing my line.

"My NAME is Joe Jeff." "MY name is Joe Jeff." "My name IS Joe Jeff." In four days I have it memorized.

At noon on Wednesday I am in the offices of Goodson-Todman. There I meet the real Joe Jeff, as well as the other imposter.

The other imposter's name is Dick Leathers. He is a 35-year-old flight attendant for TWA whose ambition is to become a commodities czar. Dick Leathers, it turns out, was raised in Greenville, Ohio. His family always took the *Daily News,* he says. You will not see his name mentioned again in this column.

Joe Jeff is 25 years old. The name of the school at which he teaches kissing is the Open University of Washington.

Open U is not a college in the accepted use of the word. I mean, it does not have a dean of engineering, a football team or a tent city. What it does have is courses in such scholastic areas as "summer sun rebirth," "bicycle repair and maintenance," and "basta pasta (101 and 102)."

A woman leads the three of us into a small office. For the next hour, we are briefed on the show's ground rules and filled in on the history of kissing.

"Report to NBC at 2:10," we are told when the briefing is finished. It is now 1:15.

My little heart is going pocketa-pocketa-pocketa.

At 2:10 we reassemble in studio 8H at NBC. Someone there decides that my tan, three-piece suit is too conservative. A minion is dispatched to find something more liberal for me to wear.

Meanwhile, a young lady leads us on a walk-through, explaining to us what we will say and where we will stand when we say it. This is followed by a camera rehearsal, with out-of-work actors filling in for the celebrity panelists.

Eventually the minion returns with the shirt he has been sent to buy for me. It is a bright red dashiki, one of those loose-fitting shirts that looks a lot like a maternity blouse.

I put it on and check myself in the mirror. Not too bad. But somewhere, I can't help thinking, there is a pregnant woman with nothing to wear.

Our show will be the last of five taped today. After the rehearsal there is nothing left to do but wait. The time is filled with conversation, cups of backstage coffee and trips to the men's room. Lots of trips to the men's room.

My little heart is going boom-biddy, boom-biddy, boom.

Finally it is our turn to go on.

The theme song plays. The lights come up. The three of us walk onto the stage and take our places. I am contestant No. 3.

My little heart is going clumpty-thud, clumpty-thud.

"No. 1," an unseen announcer demands, "what is your name, please?"

"My name is Joe Jeff."

"No. 2?"

"My name is Joe Jeff."

"And No. 3?"

No. 3. That's me. I stare into the red lights of the camera. Twelve million viewers. Every one of them waiting to hear me screw up.

My little heart is going BOOMITY-CLANG, RATTLE, RATTLE, GASP, SPUTTER, WHEEZE.

NEXT: The $116.67 misunderstanding.

The $116.67 Misunderstanding

July 16, 1977

NEW YORK—The scenario is simple.

A gentleman named Jim Trane and two gentleman pretending to be Jim Trane stand side-by-side in a television studio. At the announcer's cue, each in turn will say in a loud, clear voice:

"My name is Jim Trane."

The show begins. The announcer gives the first cue: "No. 1. What is your name, please?"

In a loud, clear voice, No. 1 answers:

"My name is Jim Pullman."

It is *To Tell The Truth's* all-time classic anecdote and the reason that it is running through my mind is because, at this very moment, I am standing in a television studio and the announcer has just given me my cue.

Fortunately, I am not contestant No. 1. I am contestant No. 3. In a loud, clear voice, I say:

"My name is Joe Jeff."

My name isn't really Joe Jeff, you understand. The real Joe Jeff is standing next to me, contestant No. 2. And his name really isn't Joe Jeff, either. It's Joe Goldblatt. But Joe Jeff is the name he uses at the Open University of Washington, D.C., where he teaches kissing. If I taught a course in kissing, I'd probably change my name, too.

In any event, for the next 15 minutes we will all pretend to be Joe Jeff, kissing professor, for the purpose of fooling the celebrity panel.

If all goes well, this show, No. 3205, will be seen by 12 million viewers sometime this fall.

To prepare for my role, I have done a great deal of research into the topic of kissing.

I know, for instance, that ancient Greeks could be put to death for kissing in public (there were equally heavy penalties for middle-aged Greeks). I know that in Bangkok, there is a $25 fine for kissing in a movie theater.

And I know that humans are not the only ones who kiss. Some animals also kiss. Birds, for example. And elephants. And snails.

I hope one of the celebrities asks me how snails kiss.

"Very slowly," I will answer.

The questioning begins. Audrey Peters, a veteran of the soap opera "Love of Life," gets the first turn.

"No. 2," she asks, "where did you get your training?"

Darn. I had an ad lib prepared for that one. "In the back seat of my father's '56 Chevy," I was going to say.

But No. 2, sounding as if he just read a book about kissing, plays it straight.

Audrey Peters turns to me.

"No. 3, what type of person do you get in your course?"

I do not have an ad lib prepared for that one. The only answer I can think of is "horny." I figure that might get bleeped. I decide to play it straight also.

"All sorts of persons," I lie, "all ages, all walks of life . . ."

The questioning continues.

Nipsey Russell asks me if alcohol had anything to do with the beginning of kissing. It is obviously a question that calls for a light-hearted answer. My rapier-like mind hesitates only a second.

"No," I quip.

Kitty Carlisle asks me about romantic kissing. I say that the course does not include romantic kissing, only social kissing.

Bill Cullen asks if it is proper, when kissing a woman's hand, to lift it up to your lips. I think back to the last time I kissed someone's hand. It was when the 4-year-old had his fingers run over by his brother's Big Wheel.

But I answer unhesitatingly, "No, that is never proper." Bill Cullen apparently swallows that, because he nods his head.

Then the questioning period is over. It is time for the voting.

Audrey Peters, for reasons that are not quite clear to anyone, especially her, votes for No. 1. Nipsey Russell also votes for No. 1. Kitty Carlisle votes for me. I have, she says, "a professional air."

Thanks to a bravura performance by No. 2, who managed to sound like a phony even when he was telling the truth, we have stumped three of the four celebrities. If Bill Cullen also votes wrong, it will be a clean sweep and the three of us will split $500.

That's $166.67 each. If he votes for No. 2, the real Joe Jeff, we get only $50 each. $116.67 is riding on his decision.

"I voted for No. 2," he says. "My beloved father-in-law has studied kissing in all the countries of this Earth and he jibes completely with what No. 2 says. When a man kisses a lady's hand, he should bend down to where her hand is."

"That was No. 3 who said that," emcee Joe Garagiola points out.

"Oh," Bill Cullen says, ". . . what's my father-in-law know?"

Bill Cullen stands by his mistaken vote, ruining our sweep and costing each of us $116.67. That's not a fortune, of course, but it would still buy a few bags of groceries and I am plenty upset about it.

The way I figure it, Bill Cullen owes me 467 boxes of macaroni and cheese.

2 Howdy Doody, Charlie McCarthy and Other Funny People

I never had a chance to meet Groucho Marx and it's too late now and I'm sorry about that.

But I have sat on the lap of Edgar Bergen and at the left hand of William F. Buckley Jr. I have discovered firsthand that Erma Bombeck is just as funny as her columns and that Jonathan Winters is just as strange as his act.

What's more, I have interviewed a witch, a pizza eating champ and a spaghetti eating chimp.

It's things like those that keep me in the newspaper business. Lord knows it isn't the money.

Howdy You Like That, Never Heard of Him

Apr. 16, 1977

When I learn that Buffalo Bob Smith is going to be in town and that I am going to be the one to interview him, I rush right home to tell the kids.

Boy, will they be impressed. They'll probably all want to go along with me.

I find them in the living room, clustered around the television. They are watching a Marcus Welby rerun.

"Guess who I'm going to interview?" I ask.

"Idi Amin?"

"No. Try again."

"Michael Blumenthal?"

"Nope."

"We give up."

"How about if I give you a clue? If I say, 'Hey kids, what time is it?' what would you say?"

"4:13."

"OK, if you're going to be that way about it. The man I'm going to interview is Buffalo Bob."

"Who?"

"You know, the man who created Howdy Doody."

"Who the heck is Howdy Doodoo?"

"Not Doodoo. Doody. Howdy Doody."

"So? Who is he?"

"Well, when Daddy was a boy, Howdy Doody was a big television star."

"Mommy says they didn't have television when you were a boy."

"Mommy's just feeling catty this week because she's all out of peroxide and the gray's showing through. Anyway, Howdy Doody was a real television superstar."

"You mean like Farrah Fawcett?"

"Not exactly. You see, Howdy Doody wasn't a real person. He was artificial."

"Was he bionic?"

"No, I think he was plaster."

"Mommy says sometimes you get plastered."

"Never mind."

"What did Howdy Dowdy do, Daddy?"

"Howdy Dowdy, uh, Doody, did lots of things. He could sing and he could dance. You might say Howdy Doody did double duty."

"Did Hoody Doody do other stuff?"

"Sure. He talked to his friends."

"Who were his friends?"

"Let's see. There was Clarabell and the Flubadub and Princess Summerfallwinterspring and . . ."

"Wait a minute. You want to run those by us again? Did you say Clarabell, Flubadub and Princess Whatsername?"

"Summerfallwinterspring."

"Yeah, that one. You mean to say you watched a show like that and then you have the nerve to tell us that *Scooby Doo, Dynomutt* is a stupid show?"

"But, Howdy Doody's show was really neat. Phineas T. Bluster was always being mean and Clarabell blew his horn a lot and Chief Thunderthud ran around saying 'Kowabunga' and . . . hey, where are you kids going?"

"It's time for *Brady Bunch*."

So when it is time to interview Buffalo Bob before his appearance at Sinclair College yesterday, I go alone. What do they know about good television, anyway?

Buffalo Bob is 59 years old now, but he doesn't look a whole lot different than he did when the original show went off the air in 1960.

Howdy Doody, on the other hand, has changed a lot. The original Howdy Doody is retired and has been replaced on the new show that is seen in many parts of the country.

The old Howdy began as just a voice on Bob Smith's *Triple B Ranch* radio show in 1946. When Buffalo Bob and Howdy moved to television the following year, network executives alertly decided that a body was needed to go with the voice. Even in 1947, kids weren't interested in watching a man talk to himself.

Some strings were pulled and Disney Studios in California

was commissioned to create a puppet to match Bob Smith's Howdy Doody voice.

The show lasted 13 years and nearly 3,000 performances—and plenty of highlights.

Once a member of the Peanut Gallery interrupted a national Tootsie Roll commercial to tell Buffalo Bob that he was allergic to chocolate.

And there was the inevitable time that a kid tugged on Buffalo Bob's fringed jacket during a Halloween show to alert him to the fact that he had to tinkle.

"Over there," Buffalo Bob whispered, pointing to the studio rest room. Unfortunately, the kid thought he was pointing to one of the lighted jack o'lanterns used to decorate the set.

The kid, as Buffalo Bob phrases it, put out the candle.

I learn a lot of things during our interview.

I learn that Buffalo Bob started as a singer at the age of 15 with a Buffalo group called the HiHatters.

I learn that the first Clarabell went on to become Captain Kangaroo.

I learn that he doesn't bring Howdy Doody with him for his appearances because it would require far too much equipment.

When the interview is over, all of my questions are answered. Except one.

Who the heck is Michael Blumenthal?

He's a Chimp, but Not a Chump

May 21, 1977

Frankly, I don't really believe that Kokomo Jr. is a chimpanzee. I suspect that he is really an ugly midget who is badly in need of a depilatory.

If you believe the press information put out by the Towne Mall near Middletown, which is where he is appearing through tomorrow, Kokomo Jr. is a chimpanzee.

And not just any chimpanzee either.

According to the press information, Kokomo Jr. is the world's wealthiest chimp, a millionaire with a long list of television appearances, his own account in a North Carolina bank and partnerships in 26 firms.

All of which may or may not be true.

I only know that when I meet him he is not at all interested in the banana I offer him.

"Why doesn't he want the banana," I ask his partner, Nick Carrado.

According to the press information, Nick Carrado is a millionaire, with a long list of television appearances, his own account in a North Carolina bank and partnerships in 26 firms.

"Actually," Nick Carrado says, "he doesn't particularly like bananas."

Sitting in the chair next to him, Kokomo Jr. nods his head. He is wearing a checked suit, a yellow bow tie, socks, slippers and an expensive looking watch. He is sucking on a red lollipop. I am not impressed. Kojak imitations are a dime a dozen.

"Well, if he doesn't eat bananas, what does he eat?" I ask Nick Carrado.

"His favorite is spaghetti and meatballs."

It is at this point that my keen reporter's instinct, honed by years of training and thousands of hours of research, comes to the fore.

I mean, I have seen maybe a million and a half Tarzan movies and not once did I notice Cheetah sitting in a tree eating a plate of spaghetti and meatballs.

I confront Nick Carrado with this evidence.

"He doesn't eat spaghetti and meatballs as a steady diet," he hedges. "He eats shrimp sometimes. But mainly he eats fruit and vegetables."

It is obvious that Nick Carrado is experienced in dealing with investigative reporters and will not be easily trapped. He deftly handles question after question as I try to get him to admit that Kokomo Jr. is a simian impersonator.

Through it all, Kokomo Jr. sits quietly in the chair next to him. Occasionally he throws me a kiss. I am not impressed. Dinah Shore imitations are a dime a dozen.

I try another approach.

"If Kokomo Jr. really is a chimp, let's see him swing from a vine," I challenge.

Nick Carrado looks at me blankly. I have him now.

"Swing from a vine?" he screams, looking around him at

the conference room in which the interview is being conducted.

"We're in the middle of a conference room in a brand new mall. Who the heck puts vines in a conference room?"

"Oh. Yeah. Well, maybe he could swing from an intercom wire."

"This is ridiculous," Nick Carrado says. "C'mon, Koko, we're getting out of here."

I stop them as they start to rise.

"Geez, Mr. Carrado, I'm sorry. I guess I shouldn't have given you the third degree like that. It's just that, well, in this business you've got to be skeptical. You know what I mean?"

"I understand," Nick Carrado says. "No hard feelings. Right, Koko?"

Kokomo Jr. stares at me, silently, his eyes filled with suspicion. It occurs to me that, throughout the entire 45-minute interview, Kokomo Jr. has not said even one word. I am not impressed. John Wysong imitations are a dime a dozen.

"Hey, Koko, give D.L. your autograph," Nick Carrado suggests, breaking the silence.

"You mean he can write?" I ask.

"Sure," Nick Carrado says. "His signature on a check is good anywhere. All they have to do is call his bank in North Carolina. They'll verify it."

Now I am impressed. My signature on a check isn't good anywhere.

I give Kokomo Jr. my pen and my notebook. A few seconds later he hands them back. I look down at the page he has signed.

What I see is nothing more than scratches and scrawls, totally illegible scribbling that no one could possibly read.

That clinches it. Kokomo Jr. isn't a chimpanzee at all. He's a short hairy doctor.

A Funny Thing Happened on the Way to the Septic Tank   Oct. 23, 1976

"It started with me writing a column like Heloise. You know, little household hints. Like, 'If you want to get rid of bad odors in the kitchen . . . stop cooking.'

"Then I tried more serious columns. Things like, 'Would the Pope approve of garlic as a birth control device?' "

Which is not exactly the way it started at all.

But then, as Erma Bombeck admits:

"I lie a lot.

"The basic premise of what I write is true," she explains. "But then I take it one step beyond."

And taking it one step beyond has made Erma Bombeck the most successful former obituary writer in *Journal Herald* history.

It has put her column in 601 newspapers, from San Juan to Dublin. It has spawned four books. A network television contract. Guest shots at the right hand of Johnny Carson. Closets full of honors, the latest of which is the University of Dayton Distinguished Alumnus Award which she is scheduled to receive today.

And it has made possible an all-expenses paid trip to Columbus, Ohio, which is where I catch up with her last week in the midst of an extensive tour to promote her newest book.

"I'm selling it door-to-door. I also have a line of vanilla that's going very well."

Columbus is a typical stop on a schedule that has her in Detroit one day, Minneapolis the next and home to Paradise Valley, Ariz., only on weekends.

"My kids think I'm the Avon Lady."

At 8:45 in the morning she walks from the Neil House hotel, where her name is on the marquee, around the corner to the Ohio Theater, where her name is on the marquee.

Later in the morning she will be the first speaker of the season in a series of lectures sponsored by the Columbus Symphony Orchestra Women's Assn. But first there is a backstage press conference.

Radio statio WBNS is there. The *Ohio State Lantern* is there. The *Columbus Dispatch*, which carries her column, is there. The *Columbus Citizen Journal*, which doesn't carry her column, is not there.

Despite the title of her lecture—"Call Me Ms-erable"—she admits in answer to a question that she is not women's lib-oriented.

"I'm aware that a lot of women out there are fighting my battles for me and I appreciate it," she says. "I just don't buy the whole package."

It is one of the few serious things she will say in public today. Mostly her answers are smooth and easy, developed over 12 years of hearing basically the same questions.

"I'm 49. The reason I volunteer my age so readily is that I look 53."

"I don't think anything I've written has offended my husband or my children. At least, that's what their lawyers say."

"Yes, we've always had dogs. We give them human names. Like Murray, Jack, Kate. Then there are the kids: Spot and Rover and . . ."

Conversations with Erma Bombeck seldom go more than a few minutes without laughter. People who knew her when her name was a household word only in her own household say that she has alway suffered from a chronic inability to remain serious for very long.

They cite the time during World War II when she was a high school student at Patterson and a part-time copy girl with the *Dayton Herald* and she wrote the obituary of enormously popular local columnist Marj Heyduck. It was a good effort, too, even if it was 25 years premature.

And they remember the five years she spent in *The Journal Herald* Modern Living section, where she really did write a Heloise-type column. Only it was called *Operation: Dustrag* and women who read it never did find out how to combat waxy yellow buildup.

She left the paper in 1953 to settle down in Centerville with a former *Journal Herald* sports writer, who later became the principal at Roth High School.

"I left to have a baby. For the next 12 years I didn't write anything but bad checks and grocery lists. After awhile I realized that I did not feel fulfilled when the highlight of my day was visiting the meat in my food locker.

"But what do you do when you're too old for a paper route . . . too young for Social Security . . . too clumsy to steal . . . and too tired for an affair?"

She began writing a once a week humor column for the

Kettering-Oakwood Times, commenting on the things she knew best: Diapers, septic tanks, car pools, kids.

"Children should be judged on what they are — a punishment from God."

A year later she was brought back to *The Journal Herald* by Editor Glenn Thompson. Her first column dealt with kids' allowances.

"We doled out 15 cents a week until we were awarded the 'Chintzy Employer of the Month' award on our block. A grievance committee informed us our children could make more in a Chinese rice paddy."

Three months later her column was offered for syndication. A paper in Fort Worth was the first taker. In two years 38 papers were running the column and her first book, *At Wit's End,* was out.

The Bombeck family was on its way out of what she called "the hamburger days." It moved to Bellbrook. It moved again, this time to Arizona.

A second book, *Just Wait Till You Have Children of Your Own,* was published. And a third, *I Lost Everything in the Post-Natal Depression.*

The newest book, for which she received a $110,000 advance, is called *The Grass Is Always Greener over the Septic Tank,* and is based, she says, on her days in Centerville.

"I was on tour for three weeks and the minute I got home and walked in the door the phone was ringing. It was a neighbor, who wanted to know where I get my septic tank cleaned."

The new book is the most successful yet, with 150,000 hard cover sales and eighth place on the *New York Times* list. Trips to Columbus, Ohio, are a large part of the reason.

So Erma Bombeck concludes the press conference and walks onto the stage of the wondrously-gilded Ohio Theater, where she is introduced as "Erma Brombeck."

For an hour and 10 minutes she is a low-key Joan Rivers, devastating an audience of 2,500 with anecdotes, column excerpts and middle-aged wives tales that go one step beyond.

"My mother never told me that the high spot of my day

would be taking the knots out of shoelaces with my teeth . . .
that a kid had wet on all day."

"You show me a woman who volunteers and I will show
you a husband with a pin in his underwear."

"Do you have any idea what it's like to travel on a vacation
with a daughter who has kidneys the size of lentils?"

After the lecture there are autographs to sign and after the
autographs there is a mini-cam interview with Channel 10.

Then there is a luncheon back at the Neil House with 475
women who have paid $7.50 to eat chicken and ask questions.

"Does your husband have pins in his underwear?"

"I haven't seen his underwear in so long . . ."

"What are the names and ages of your children?"

"There's Betsy, who is 23. Andy, 21. And Matt, 18. Matt is
the poster child this month for planned parenthood."

When the questions run out it is pushing 2 o'clock and she
has to get ready to catch the 3:26 flight back to Arizona, where
she will spend the weekend catching up on her writing.

"The first thing that will happen is that my son will meet
me at the airport and say, 'When are you going to the store?'

"Then, when I get home, I'll change the toilet paper spin-
dles that haven't been changed all week and I'll . . ."

Watch Out for Witches and Lance Collins

Sept. 6, 1975.

It should be noted at the beginning that I do not believe in
ghosts, goblins, sea monsters, little green men, Easter bunnies or
elves who make cookies in the trunks of trees.

Which is not to say that Lance Collins is not a witch.

I mean, if Lance Collins says he is a witch (or, rather, a
wizard, which is what you call a male witch) who am I to
argue?

The problem is, Lance Collins does not at all look the way
the Brothers Grimm and I think a witch should look. His nose
does not hook and his fingernails aren't long and curved and
there are no black gaps between his teeth. If he has a wart on his
chin, it is well covered by his neat brownish beard.

But Lance Collins says that he has practiced witchcraft for a majority of his 26 years and, what's more, there are 5,000 practicing witches in Dayton, which he says is "a very witchy city."

It is possible, of course, that Lance Collins is merely saying such things to promote interest in his newly opened store on North Main Street: The Witches Caldron. However, that does not prove that witches do not exist. There are, after all, half a dozen religious bookstores in the Dayton area, but no one disputes the existence of Christians and Jews.

And witchcraft is, by any definition, a religion. It comes complete with priests and priestesses, prayers and chants, rites and sects, and a diety named Diana. It has just about everything that other religions have, with the possible exception of bingo.

What witchcraft does not have is followers who worship Satan.

"Witchcraft has nothing to do with Satanism," Lance Collins insists. "This is the kind of thing that a lot of preachers are saying because witchcraft is the most rapidly growing religion today and they don't like that. When this story comes out, every preacher in town will be trying to get on TV and radio to attack us."

Although he says some Roman Catholic clergymen have shown a tolerance towards witchcraft, Lance Collins has encountered mainly hostility from most Christian denominations. Understandably, Lance Collins does not speak kindly of them. Referring to one well-known Christian evangelist who brings his crusades to Dayton periodically, he says: "I know for a fact that he is a bi-sexual. What's more, he doesn't even believe in Jesus."

Lance Collins says he has done three "black spells" in his life. One was on a minister in San Antonio.

"He came up and slapped a young girl who was our high priestess . . . that's the kind of love they're always talking about. So on Halloween we got some hairs from his hairbrush and made a doll and stuck pins in it. A week later he had a heart attack."

(Black spell dolls, incidentally, are available at The Witches Caldron for $5. You provide your own hairs.)

With: The other dummy and Edgar; William Buckley, the columnist on his right; and Erma, whose kids think she's the Avon Lady. Also: King of the Cowboys, Mr. Wunnerful, and the weird Mr. Winters.

Despite the unpleasantness with the minister in San Antonio, Lance Collins says that witchcraft basically is a peaceful religion, operating under the guideline of "do what you will as long as it harms no one." He claims that the powers of witchcraft have been used to achieve favorable weather, heal the sick, find jobs for the unemployed and stem a rash of killings that a fortune teller had predicted would plague Dayton.

What's more, he says, it was a concentrated effort by witches that helped bring about the U.S. disengagement in Vietnam. Which is something else Richard Nixon didn't tell us.

Of course, a witch is only as good as his raw materials. And

The Witches Caldron, Lance Collins declares, carries nothing but the highest quality bloodroot, exorcism incense and graveyard dust.

Many of the items on the store's shelves are for sexuality.

"Sex is about 50 percent of witchcraft," he says. "There's no such thing as a virgin witch. That's why we don't have any tense and cranky witches."

Lance Collins' first spell, in fact, was cast at the age of 10 or 11 on a girl of 14 whom he knew but wanted to know better. If there's anyone you'd like to know better, or more often, Lance recommends Venus perfume ($5 an ounce), which contains vervain, verbena and patchouli. He can't guarantee it, but he can tell you some pretty good stories about it.

Lance Collins hopes to have $50,000 worth of stock by Halloween, all of it protected by a magic spell he has placed on his shop. ("It won't keep burglars out, but I feel sorry for any who do break in.")

And he envisions big things for witchcraft in Dayton, including more covens, maybe a witch museum and perhaps even a witch college.

I can see it now. It's a Saturday afternoon in some future fall. It is the big game: Witch U vs. Notre Dame. Chris Schenkel is saying: "Keep your eye on No. 13 for Witch U. He can really fly. I mean, really."

It Takes a Dummy to Interview One

Mar. 24, 1977

Confounding the critics who predicted they would eventually separate and seek individual careers, Edgar Bergen and Charlie McCarthy are into their sixth decade as a comedy team.

Their inimitable timing, perfected through long hours of practicing together, remains flawless, as they proved here last week in a pair of Town Hall lecture series appearances.

And, no matter what you may have read, Charlie McCarthy's lips do not move when Edgar Bergen talks.

After their first show at Memorial Hall, I dropped in backstage to catch the press conferences conducted by the two durable comedians.

Bergen, 74, is somewhat heavier and a great deal grayer than he was as a vaudevillian fresh out of Northwestern University in the early '20s. McCarthy, on the other hand, has managed to retain his youthful appearance. He is 54 years old, but he does not look a day over 11.

Although McCarthy does most of the talking onstage, it is Bergen who fields the questions during the press conference. McCarthy, meanwhile, sits on the floor in a corner of the dressing room. If he has any reaction to the questions being asked, he gives no outward indication. Throughout the proceedings, his face remains expressionless, a wooden mask.

Seeing him there that way, alone and virtually ignored, it strikes me as curious that McCarthy, by far the wittier of the duet, seldom is interviewed alone. I cannot think of one instance in which I have seen McCarthy interviewed without Bergen at his side.

When the press conference has ended and Bergen moves outside the dressing room to pack up his gear, McCarthy makes no move to follow. Soon, only the two of us are in the room

My every journalistic instinct tells me this is my big chance. But what if McCarthy is like Sinatra and hates reporters? On the other hand, what's to fear from a 20-pound fiber glass dummy who wears a monocle?

"Er, excuse me, Mr. McCarthy, I'm from *The Journal Herald.* I guess maybe you don't like to be interviewed, but . . ."

"Wait a minute, kid. Who told you that?"

"Well, nobody. But I've never seen you quoted anywhere, so I just naturally assumed . . ."

"Listen, kid, I'll tell you why you never see me quoted. It's because a long time ago Bergen spread it around that I was too stupid to answer questions. You know, a real dummy."

"You mean, you're not a dummy?"

"Do you usually go around interviewing dummies?"

"Well, only when the regular politics writer is sick. But, getting back to what you were saying, it sounds like you and Mr. Bergen don't get along too well. I always thought you had a great relationship."

"That's what everybody thought before Cher dumped Sonny. The truth is, I'm getting pretty fed up with Bergen."

"Why? Is he tough to work with?"

"Tough? You have no idea. Every show it's the same thing. We come out onstage, he sticks his hand up the back of my coat and says something like: 'Well, Charlie, how are you feeling today?' How's that for a grabber? He throws me a stupid line like that and I'm supposed to come up with something funny. After 54 years, I'm sick of it."

"I suppose that would be tough."

"You better believe it. And I'll tell you something else. I'm not too crazy about some of the other people in this show, either."

"Really?"

"Nope. Like, on the road I always get stuck rooming with Mortimer Snerd. You know, the kid with the overbite. I keep telling him, they got dentists that can fix him up. But he says he's happy the way he is. He says this way he doesn't have to open his mouth to brush his teeth."

"I can see where you might be a little annoyed. But, really, those don't sound like good reasons for breaking up such a successful act."

"They don't huh? Well, I'll tell you what, Dale. I'll trade jobs with you for awhile. You go sit on Bergen's lap and I'll pound your typewriter."

"Well, gee, I'd like to, Mr. McCarthy, but I'm not sure how my bosses would go for that. I mean, how are they gonna react if they look back at my desk and see a dummy writing my column?"

"Who's gonna notice?"

King of the Cowboys Still Packs 'Em In

Aug. 26, 1975

COLUMBUS — It has been 21 years since Roy Rogers last proved that it is possible to punch out an entire gang of movie desperados without having your white hat fall off, but there still seems to be magic in the name.

How else can you explain the crowds that overflowed the grandstand and planted their oceans of folding chairs all over the infield for his two shows at the Ohio State Fair Sunday?

"I don't think he's part of the nostalgia thing," insists hard-driving Art Rush, who has been Roy Rogers' agent for 33 years. "He never stopped being popular. Never. He still gets about 3,500 letters a week. Last year he got 20,000 letters from Ghana, Africa, when one of his pictures was shown there. That's G-H-A-N-A."

In addition to being a nifty speller, Art Rush has an agent's flair for overstatement on behalf of his client. Rogers himself puts the current letter count at "a couple of hundred a day."

Petty discrepancies like 2,100 letters a week don't concern Rush, who spews out evidences of his client's continuing popularity faster than you can fan your six-gun.

"He just flew in on a private jet from Texas where he finished his latest movie yesterday," Rush said as he waited for Rogers to emerge from his trailer-dressing room behind the grandstand stage. "It's called *Mackintosh and T.J.* It's a big one . . . a million dollars. He fills the house at every fair he appears in. He's got 200 restaurants with his name on them. He's got a museum in Apple Valley, Calif., a horse ranch, he's doing commercials for three major products, he's got a new series we're selling called 'Roy Rogers Presents the Great Movie Cowboys.' Put that down, that's important."

"Gosh," I said humbly after putting that down, "I didn't realize Roy was still so big. When can I talk to him?"

"You can't talk to him," Rush snapped. "He's too busy. His show starts in a few minutes and first he's got to do a promotion on television for 4-H clubs."

Sure enough, a few seconds later Roy Rogers emerged in person from his trailer-dressing room and headed directly for the TV camera. The cue card containing his message was already in place. The first line was, "Hi, I'm Roy Rogers."

At 63, Roy Rogers appears to be in remarkably good condition. He is, he says, the same 170 pounds he was 30 years ago. His brown hair is exceptionally full for a man of his age. And exceptionally brown. As he sprints from the TV camera to the stage, he shows no signs of the heart problem that struck him several years ago.

His appearance onstage is greeted by a semi-standing ovation from the crowd of 25,000. Rogers receives the reception with a wave of his white hat and waits for the noise to subside, the bright sunlight glittering on the silver fringe of his cowboy shirt.

"I'm sure glad to be back home," he says finally.

The King of the Cowboys was born in that famed frontier settlement, Cincinnati. As a youngster he moved to Duck Run, Ohio. Or, as Art Rush says it, "Duckrunpopulationfourteen." According to Rush, he spent his early years on a houseboat, which seems a curious place for a young cowboy to learn how to rope steers.

Of course, his name wasn't Roy Rogers then. It was Leonard Slye. The new name was born somewhere between Duck Run and Hollywood. It is just as well. Somehow the big fight scene wouldn't be the same with Gabby Hayes cackling: "Go get 'em, Leonard."

Perhaps because the years have treated him so kindly, Rogers makes a point of telling the audience he is 63. There is applause for that. There is even more applause when he announces that he has 15 grandchildren. I have never been able to understand why audiences applaud things like that. Being a grandfather is, after all, a rather indirect accomplishment.

For 15 minutes Rogers mixes a little patter with a little music.

He plugs his upcoming movie: "Trying to find a picture these days that is decent enough for Trigger to see is pretty hard." The audience applauds. "I promise you that this picture will be the kind you won't be embarrassed to take your children to, your grandmother to, or even your dog to."

He plugs his museum. "We've got Trigger there, stuffed and mounted real nice. I told Dale that when I die she can just skin me and put me right up there on top of him."

He acknowledges his musical group, The Sons of the Pioneers, who have enough miles on them now to be called The Grandfathers of the Pioneers.

Then he introduces his wife, Dale Evans, who was known as Frances Octavia Smith when she was growing up in Texas. It is a fact of human life that time usually deals more gently with the male of the species in terms of outward appearances. Such is the case in the Rogers family. In 1955, there was not quite so much Dale Evans for Buttermilk to carry around.

Dale Evans leans heavily to gospel singing and flag waving, both of which go over well here. It is not until she leaves the stage that she is informed that she omitted a small part of her routine: she was supposed to introduce her stepson.

"They've been so busy," Art Rush explains. "They didn't have time to rehearse. Did I tell you they just flew in from doing a movie in Texas?"

Dale's oversight is corrected by Roy when he reappears on the stage.

"I had two sons," he says. "We called the oldest one Dusty and the second one Sandy. If I had a third one, I guess I would have called him Filthy."

Roy "Dusty" Rogers Jr. is 28, with blond hair and a very good baritone voice. It is better, in fact than his father's ever was.

But Roy Rogers Jr. will never be as famous as his father. Kids these days don't believe in white hats.

Hi-yo, Aluminum. . . Away!

June 18, 1977

When I learn that the Lone Ranger is in town visiting 7-Eleven stores, I am not really impressed.

After all, masked men dropping in on 7-Elevens is not all that unusual.

On the other hand, I have often wondered why the Lone Ranger and his faithful Indian companion were always in such a hurry to ride off together into the sunset. Is it something Anita Bryant should know about?

So the other day, I mosey out to one of the stores where Clayton Moore, television's Lone Ranger, is appearing on behalf of muscular dystrophy. When I arrive, he is sitting in front of the store, signing autographs and encouraging kids to collect money in their neighborhoods for MD.

At 62, Clayton Moore still appears capable of clearing out the saloon, wiping out the rustlers and stamping out the range war without having his white hat fall off. His body is still trim.

His mask is still unwrinkled.

Clayton Moore was television's Lone Ranger for 200 episodes, from 1949 through 1956. He is proud of the fact that in none of those episodes did he ever kill a guy, kiss a gal or say "ain't."

"We were always very careful about grammar," Clayton Moore says. "There's more strength in perfect grammar than there is in slang."

I am surprised by that statement, but I make a mental note to remember it. I also make a mental note never to tangle with Roz Young.

To a generation whose heroes include Thor, Howard the Duck and Shang Chi (master of Kung Fu), the Lone Ranger is not a household name. Many kids, he admits, call him the "Long Ranger." The more knowledgeable are aware that he used to ride around with an Indian named "Toronto."

But the parents remember.

"I started listening to the show when it was on radio," says a woman of 39 who has stopped by to meet Clayton Moore. "I'd sit through the whole half-hour just to hear them say, 'Who was that masked man?' "

"Hey, Lone Ranger," says a hulking truck driver who parks his rig and walks up without embarrassment for an autographed picture, "I'm trying to teach my truck to rear up on its hind wheels."

"You've got to feed it Cheerios," Clayton Moore tells him.

"You know," he says after the trucker has chugged away, "my horse is still alive. He's 28 years old, now. And Jay Silverheels lives about two miles from my house in California."

Jay Silverheels was Tonto. Except in Mexico, where "tonto" is the Spanish word for "stupid." On Mexican television, Jay Silverheels was "El Toro."

But little else connected with the Lone Ranger has changed since the original radio show was created in 1933.

"He's still the same basic character," Clayton Moore says of the heroic role he has played for 28 years. "Honest. Decent. A wonderful example for kids. He never shoots to kill and he never hits a man when he's down."

"Why is he the LONE Ranger," I ask. "Is it his breath, or what?"

"The Lone Ranger originally was named John Reid and he was one of six Texas Rangers caught in an ambush," Clayton Moore relates. "The other five were killed and he was badly wounded and left for dead.

"Fortunately, an Indian whose life he had saved when they were both boys came along and found him, nursing him back to health. Can you guess who that Indian was?"

"Sasheen Littlefeather?"

"No. It was Tonto."

The Lone Ranger became Tonto's "kemo sabay," the Potawatomi term for "good buddy." For more than 20 years, they rode the West, shooting bad guys in the shoulder and littering the frontier with silver bullets.

Clayton Moore carries on the silver bullet tradition to this day, leaving one in each town he visits. Sometimes he leaves one in the back of a cab. Sometimes it is in a restaurant. It's just like it was in the Lone Ranger's day. Except that Clayton Moore's silver bullets are aluminum.

"That's another thing that always puzzled me," I say. "What was the point in the Lone Ranger using silver bullets? Were there a lot of werewolves in the old West?"

"No. The reason was because his brother owned a silver mine," Clayton Moore explains. "So it was easy for him to get silver."

Then Clayton Moore turns back to the crowd of Lone Ranger fans who have gathered around his table, leaving me to reflect upon how neatly things work out sometimes.

What if the Lone Ranger's brother had owned a pig farm?

"Say, who was that masked man, anyway?"

"I don't know, but he left this behind."

"Why, it's . . ."

"Yep. A pork chop."

Fastest Pizza Eater in the World

May 27, 1975

NORWALK, Ohio — It is not necessarily correct to say that "Mush Mouth" Pacetti ATE an entire pizza in 28 seconds here Sunday.

Actually, what he did was cram sections of a nine-inch pizza into a six-inch mouth and then wash down the unchewed mess with sips of water. That may sound revolting, but in reality it is merely disgusting.

But then, 21-year-old Mariano "Mush Mouth" Pacetti never claimed to be the world's neatest pizza eater. Only the fastest. None who saw him perform here in the World Pizza Eating Championship will dispute his claim.

Norwalk has Rick Reiff to blame for the World Pizza Eating Championship. Rick Reiff, in addition to being a reporter for the *Norwalk Reflector,* is president of PIG (Patrons of Imbibation and Gastronomy). Given the assignment of coming up with something novel for Norwalk's Memorial Day weekend festival, he suggested an eating contest.

"Eating is something that dates as far back as the beginning of the human race," Reiff pointed out. "Even further, because the dinosaurs did it, too."

Dazzled by such a lucid grasp of history, the festival committee OK'd the contest.

What made Reiff's concept novel is that it stressed speed rather than endurance.

"Our format is more conducive to the good, little man," he explained. "Most eating records are based on how much a person can eat over an extended period of time, which virtually restricts them to persons who are built like houses. There's nothing more boring than watching a guy eat until he can't belch anymore."

Reiff was also struck by the realization that the Guinness Book of Records, which includes listings for frankfurter eating (20 two-ounce franks, without buns, in 4:47), doughnut downing (37 in 15 minutes) and spaghetti swallowing (288 yards), had no pizza eating record.

A call to the Guinness people in New York produced assurance that the winner of the Norwalk contest would be considered for the next edition of that compendium of human follies.

All that remained, then, was to enlist Northern Ohio's most renowned pizza eater, "Mush Mouth" Pacetti. For $50, he agreed to bring his mouth to Norwalk.

"Mush Mouth" wasn't always famous. He used to be just another guy, hanging around burger joints in Cleveland, doing nothing more spectacular than eating Whoppers in one bite.

All that is changed now, of course. Now he is the world pizza eating champion and his name may wind up in Guinness and get as famous as Hoolihan and Big Chuck.

Hoolihan and Big Chuck are Cleveland television stars, with their own weekend monster movie show at night. Between reels of "The Blob that Ate Kansas City" they poke fun at Parma and tell jokes about a certain ethnic group and feature such guests as "Mush Mouth" Pacetti.

Although "Mush Mouth" once consumed a pizza on camera in 28 seconds, the performances that people talk about most are the ones he lost. Like the two times he was beaten by the Hungry Hungarian.

"That bleeper cheated," "Mush Mouth" says of Mr. Hungarian. "He dropped a crust this big on the floor and nobody saw it. Hey, I've dropped pieces lots of times, but I always picked them up and ate them."

"Mush Mouth" has no alibis about his loss to a German Shepherd, but points out, "they starved that dog for two days. You just don't do that to a German Shepherd. I was supposed to shake hands with him before the match and he snapped at my fingers."

As a result of nearly being the eatee instead of the eater, "Mush Mouth" has vowed never to compete against a dog again. Fortunately for all concerned, a German Shepherd and a Great Dane originally scheduled to appear in the Norwalk contest were withdrawn due to objections by the local Humane Society. Also forced to pull out was Capt. Stanley Wells of the Salvation Army, whose plan was to cut his pizza into 25 pieces and down a piece a second.

Still, there were 16 challengers for "Mush Mouth," including 200-pound Herb Harkness, a defensive end on the high school football team who choked in his first practice attempt; 165-pound wrestler Don Leto, whose best training camp time was 0:42; and 25-year-old Clarence Case, who boasted he would shatter the 25-second barrier.

The pizzas, made to strict specifications (four ounces of dough, two ounces of sauce, two ounces of cheese), were provided by Joseppi's Real Italian Foods. They were made personally by the owner of Joseppi's Real Italian Foods, who is not named Joseppi and is not a real Italian. His name is Roy Kreidel and he is a real German.

"This has developed into quite a thing," said Roy Kreidel.

"I wish I was someplace else this weekend," said Mrs. Kreidel.

A crowd of more than a thousand sweltered around the flatbed truck-stage in front of Joseppi's to witness the event. It was, Roy Kreidel ventured, the biggest thing to happen in Norwalk since the high school won the State Class AA football championship last year and everybody in town drove to Dayton for the final game and some wag put a sign on the courthouse that said "Will the last one out of town please turn off the lights?"

"Mush Mouth," a 1-3 favorite according to Rick the Italian, waited impatiently for the first heat to begin. He danced up and down, he flexed his fingers, he flexed his mouth. At the signal, the crowd began the countdown: "Four, three, two, one."

The first five contestants began cramming, but all eyes were on "Mush Mouth." His form was flawless, his hand-to-lip coordination awesome. With both hands he shoved pizza into his mouth two slices at a time. Each time he filled his mouth to overflowing he somehow found room for a sip of water. Shove, sip. Shove, sip. Dribble.

In 28 seconds he was finished and he was able to sit back and watch his gagging, bulging-cheeked challengers. Don Leto finished second in 0:43, explaining later that "I had it in my mouth first, but I couldn't get it down." Clarence Case was third at 0:50, far from his predicted time of 0:23. Herb Harkness choked again, finished with a disappointing 2:45.

When it was all over, "Mush Mouth" Pacetti stood holding

his trophy with the gold pig on top and described to the world how he ate his way to the top.

"You've got to tell yourself you've got to swallow. It's all up here," he related, tapping his forehead.

Which was not quite true, either. It wasn't all up there. Some of it was on his chin, some of it was on his T-shirt, some of it was . . .

Bill the Dill, Pickle Packing Promoter

June 7, 1975

This is, as you doubtless know, International Pickle Week. As usual, I didn't get my cards sent out on time. In fact, Pickle Week might have popped past me completely if it hadn't been for a reminder from the Pickle Packers International.

It is something of a pity to learn that the Pickle Packers' publicity person is not named Peter Piper. His name, alas, is plain old William R. Moore. He is known to his friends as Bill the Dill.

Bill the Dill has been promoting pickles practically all his life. Or, as he points out, "I've been in pickles for over 30 years."

Sometimes it can be pretty painful being a pickle pusher.

"You know how it is when your kids are in school and they ask them what their daddy does," Bill the Dill pointed out. "Well, your kids can say, 'My daddy's a journalist.' Mine always had to say, 'My pop's a pickle packer.' "

It is, indeed, a poignant picture. Perhaps even pathetic.

There are other problems in publicizing pickles. Perhaps the most pervasive is pickle prejudice. One of Bill the Dill's pet peeves pertains to St. Charles, Ill., which is the headquarters of Pickle Packers International. The pickle powers pow-wow in that pastoral place primarily because it is the central point of the 15 pickle producing nations of the free world.

At the edge of town they have signs proudly presenting St. Charles as the home of pretty, perky Karen Morrison (Miss U.S.A.) and Rick Wohlhuter, the practically peerless track and field performer. No signs are posted, however, proclaiming the presence of the pickle packers.

"It's this kind of discrimination we're fighting," says Bill the Dill, his pique coming through plainly on the phone.

"We're tired of being treated as second class vegetables. Why, did you know that more pickles are consumed in this country than canned and frozen peas put together? Obviously, were pickled tink about that, but there's much more to do.

"That's why we started Pickle Power and Pickle Liberation. Mark my words, Pickle Power will overcome."

As a first step towards overpowering the people with pickles, pickle persons make it plain that they prefer to be addressed by the non-sexist term of Ps.

"Something that really bothers us is that we're not served everywhere," says Ps. Moore. "Sure, hamburger and hot dog stands serve us. But what about the chauvinistic chicken places? So we're trying to come up with a chicken pickle or chicken relish."

Bill the Dill paused to ponder the plight of poultry without pickles. It was plain that his pique was rising to a peak of passion. It seemed perilous at that point to probe about any potential plans for promoting pickles on pizza pies.

Eventually Bill the Dill regained his poise and spoke more placidly about the plots of the Pickle Packers.

"We're also working on a seedless pickle," he pointed out. "It's sort of a forerunner to the seedless person. It will be our contribution to zero population growth."

There was another pregnant pause as the pair of us pondered the possibilities. Pictures of penniless pediatricians proliferated.

Bill the Dill has pulled off a plethora of pickle promotions in the past. Plenty of them have been peculiar.

"Two years ago, when streaking was big, we had a naked pickle streak across the public square in Charleston, S.C.," he related. "And when Henry Aaron hit his record-breaking home run, we presented him an award for poking the pill out of the park.

"The Hallmark people have a book out with a beautiful story about Super Pickle. There are pickle greeting cards and pickle puzzles and pickle putters." Presumably, Player and Palmer never have patted putts with pickle putters.

"Obviously," Bill the Dill proclaimed, "we try not to take ourselves too seriously. We take our product seriously, but not ourselves."

The pickle packers' puckish point of view periodically places them in peril. When Queen Elizabeth was promoted from princess, for instance, the Pickle Packers promulgated a pickle queen competition. The only prerequisite was that the potential potentate must be named Pickle.

"We had entries from 60 different Elizabeth Pickles," the pickle publicizer pointed out proudly. Unfortunately, the Pickle Packers also got plenty of protests from English persons who were powerfully, uh, ticked off.

"We really got in a pickle with that one," Bill the Dill put it.

Despite such pitfalls, pickle pushing is a prosperous proposition, with $525 million a year pouring in. Perennially, the public purchases and partakes of eight pounds of pickles per person. Predictably, the pickle people possess patrons in powerful places. Preeminent among them is a U.S. representative from Texas. His name is J.J. "Jake" Pickle.

Political pundits predict a promising future for Rep. Pickle. Perhaps he will rise to the country's premier public position.

President Pickle. It is a prospect to relish.

Tongue-Tied on the Left of Mr. Buckley

Jan. 11, 1977

All I can say is that anyone who would seat me next to William F. Buckley Jr. at a dinner would probably set up a blind date between Queen Juliana of the Netherlands and Billy Carter.

Sure, we're both columnists. But then, Dame Margot Fonteyn and Chesty Morgan are both dancers.

William F. Buckley's column is syndicated in more than 300 newspapers. His television show is seen each week on PBS. He is the founder of the *National Review.* In his spare time, he writes books. Among the books he has written are *God and Man at Yale; The Governor Listeth; Four Reforms — A Program for the 70s; Airborne* and *Roget's Thesaurus.*

Like Howard Cosell, William F. Buckley Jr. uses a lot of big words. The difference is, he knows what they mean.

Above all, William F. Buckley is known as the erudite, mellifluous, oxymoronic spokesman of the politically conservative.

I am known as the guy who wears pajamas with blue lions on them.

All of which I point out to the woman from the University of Dayton when she calls one day last week and invites me to a dinner being given in connection with Buckley's appearance at the school.

But, in addition to having a weird sense of humor, the woman is very persuasive and eventually I agree to show up Thursday in Room 159-60 at the Kennedy Union, which is where the dinner is being held.

When I arrive at the Kennedy Union Thursday I am met by a woman who directs me to the head table.

"You're to the left of Mr. Buckley," she says.

"Who isn't?" I reply.

Buckley arrives a few minutes later. He has just flown in from Washington, presumably on a plane with two right wings. He is wearing a gray flannel suit, pin-striped shirt and dark tie. When we are introduced, his handshake is firm.

"Very nice to meet you," he murmurs.

"Me, too," I riposte.

Then we are sitting at the head table. On Buckley's right, in the physical sense, is Father Roesch, the UD president. They chat for awhile, their conversation punctuated with genteel laughter and a sprinkling of Latin phrases.

After a while, Buckley turns to me. This is the moment I have been dreading. The moment I will have to go one-on-one with one of the foremost debaters of our time.

"When does your column appear?" he asks. Typical debater's trick. Hit your adversary with a tough one right off the bat.

But I manage to get through the first exchange without entirely disgracing myself and I start to gain confidence. After all, I tell myself, I've got a college degree, too. And we're both columnists. We probably have a great deal in common.

I decide to take the initiative.

"How much mail do you get about your column?" I ask.

"I'd estimate approximately 600 letters," he says.

"That many, huh? I don't get quite that many myself. Maybe 150, 175 a year."

"I meant 600 a week," he says.

"Oh." That stops me for a second. I'm only glad I exaggerated about the 175.

"I find that most of my negative mail comes after columns concerning religion," Buckley adds. "Which of your columns generate the most adverse letters?"

"Well, people got pretty riled up that time I wrote about dead canaries."

"Really."

I try again.

"Is there any certain place where you like to go to do your writing?" I ask.

"I spend two months every year in Switzerland," he says. "I use a friend's chalet. How about yourself?"

"Oh, well, I usually go down to the basement. It's pretty nice down there, except when the sump pump's running. Of course, when somebody upstairs flushes the toilet you can really hear it shooting down through the pipes."

I start to tell Buckley about the column I had on fixing the leak in the bathroom sink, but suddenly he turns back in his chair to talk with Father Roesch and I never do get another chance to speak with him.

Too bad. I was going to see if he wanted to be in a hamburger eating contest with me next month.

Mr. Wunnerful Charms a Cynic

June 12, 1976

What is there left to be said about Lawrence Welk? The wits, the cynics, the worshippers at the electronically amplified fountain of youth have said it all.

The Squire of Square Music, they scoff. The King of Musical Corn. An old man playing old music for old people. And uh-one and uh-two and turn off the bubble machine-uh. Pat Boone's father. John Denver's grandfather.

Well, Mr. Wunnerful and his Champagne Music Makers

came to town Thursday night. They brought their instruments, their dimples, their goodness, descending upon the University of Dayton Arena with their wash-and-wear smiles, like a band of Jimmy Carters.

And I joined them. Joined them not because I am a fan of goodness, but because I, too, am a cynic, suspicious of people who smile a lot. I always figured that people who smile a lot are hiding something. Billy James Hargis probably smiled a lot.

If I hang around backstage, I reasoned, I will find them out. Larry Hooper smoking a joint. Myron Floren with a bottle hidden in his accordion. Bobby giving Cissy a rap in the mouth.

Forty minutes before show time they begin to drift into the arena through the back entrance. Directed by signs that say, "Lawrence Welk Dressing Rooms . . . Boys . . . Girls," although some of them haven't been boys or girls for quite some time.

They are all neat and sparkly, the "girls" wholesomely good looking, the "boys" beardless, with only an occasional well-trimmed mustache.

Lawrence Welk runs a tight, Puritan ship, I have heard, complete with a man whose job it is to make sure that no double entendres slip into the lyrics. By reputation, he is the Paul Brown of television. No booze, no sex, lights out at 10.

I ask some of the performers about this as we stand around backstage.

"Oh, no, it's nothing like that," says Bobby, the dancer. I'm not sure what Bobby's last name is. I think it's Andcissy.

"At the beginning of the season he'll send us each a letter, sort of a pep talk thing," Bobby says. "But that's about all."

"Lawrence Welk is a believer in God," says a trumpet player named John, "and this permeates through the group. He has no restrictions on us, though. I think it's just that the people we have aren't the kind who would go out and get into trouble."

My conversation with John is interrupted by a man who asks if I'd like to interview Welk now. It is an opportunity I had not anticipated, at least not 20 minutes before show time. Stars are always busy before a show, too busy to talk to newspapermen. Elvis Presley has been too busy for 20 years. Frank Sinatra has been too busy all his life.

But Lawrence Welk, reputedly the second richest man in

show business with a fortune estimated as high as $50 million, is not too busy. He seems almost glad to see us, the photographer and I, when we enter his small dressing room. I have never met a star who seemed glad to see me.

He shakes my hand, this 73-year-old, self-made millionaire, and he asks me to sit down and before I can say much of anything he offers me an autographed picture.

"Well, OK," I say, "I'll give it to my mother-in-law, she's a big fan of yours." Which is a cruel kind of compliment, implying as it does that I am not a fan of his.

But Welk takes no offense as he produces a picture of himself standing on a golf course and signs the back of it. "To Ruth, your t.v. friend, Lawrence Welk."

"How about you?" he asks the photographer.

The photographer, who is young and whose musical tastes probably run more toward Led Zeppelin, clearly is not eager for an autographed photo of Lawrence Welk.

"Take one," Welk urges. "You can give it to your mom." The photographer takes one.

Having gone through newspaper clippings earlier in the day, I already know everything I care to about Lawrence Welk. I know, for instance, that he was born in North Dakota in 1903. That his first band was a six-piece group called Lawrence Welk's Hotsy Totsy Boys. That ABC received 900,000 protest letters when it canceled his show in 1971.

Because I already know these things, and because I had not expected to interview him, I do not have any intelligent questions to ask. So I ask a couple of semi-intelligent ones and, after he has answered them, I start to leave.

"Don't go," he says. "Stay around. Ask me some more questions. Here, take one of my cards, so if you're ever in California you can come and see me." He hands me a card. He hands the photographer a card.

So I ask a couple more questions that are even less intelligent than the ones before. And finally it is three minutes before show time and Lawrence Welk is apologizing because he has to leave the dressing room now.

"Here," he says, "take one of these." He hands me a key

chain, with his name imprinted on a tiny knife that hangs from it. He hands one to the photographer.

Then he is leaving the dressing room, walking toward the stage, to where 7,700 mostly old people are waiting to hear an old man's old music.

The Squire of Squares. The King of Corn. But, more than that, the kind of man who can make life awful tough for us cynics.

But You Break Up When You See Him

Nov. 13, 1976

When I encounter Jonathan Winters last Monday he is eating ice and talking about pro football.

"I didn't get to play pro," he is telling the guy who hands out soft drinks in the press box at Riverfront Stadium where the Bengals are playing the Rams. "I got tackled hard in Middletown."

The guy who hands out the soft drinks laughs so hard at this that he nearly spills the Sprite.

"I was almost crippled in Ironton," Winters continues. "And I was brought down hard in Mansfield. My helmet was on wrong."

The guy who hands out soft drinks is quivering with laughter now and any minute he is going to drop his Dr. Pepper and it is then I realize that interviewing Jonathan Winters does not necessarily mean I am going to wind up with material for a funny column.

Because the humor of a man who says his hobby is "kicking naked fish" is not meant to be strained through a typewriter. Like others of his ilk — Don Rickles, Prof. Irwin Corey, Gov. James Rhodes — Jonathan Winters is an audiovisual comic who does not need sense to make you laugh.

Still, it is not every day you get a chance to talk with a guy who titles one of his paintings *Two Birds Watching Doris Day's Cat and Dog Drown.* A guy who once had a job at WING during which he interviewed George Washington, used bait salesmen and visiting undertakers from Akron.

So while the guy who hands out soft drinks is still cracking

up over the Coke, I introduce myself to Jonathan Winters, em-
phasizing the fact that I am from the town where he was born.

"I lived in Springfield," he says. Behind me, the soft drink
guy is practically passing out in the Pepsi. I make a mental note
to remember that line. Maybe I can work it into a speech
sometime when I need a laugh.

"I spent half my life in Dayton and the other half in
Springfield. Last time I was back there, I ran into an old friend.
Wally. He wanted to know if I was still living out on
Elmwood."

Jonathan Winters slips into his Elwood P. Suggins voice.

"You still out there, Jon?"

"No, no, I'm not there anymore."

"Livin' out with your folks on St. Paris Pike then, huh?"

"Folks are dead."

"Well, where are you living?"

"I'm out in California now, Wally."

"California, huh? Watcha doin' out there?"

"I'm in teevee."

"The hell you are. Say, Ruth Ann's got a Zenith. I wonder
if you'd come over and take a look at it."

When Jonathan Winters has finished telling his Wally
story, I ask him what he is doing here in the press box at
Riverfront Stadium. I have to sort of shout the question, because
the soft drink guy is laughing so hard now that his Fresca is
starting to foam.

"I flew in with the Rams. I follow them pretty close, but
I'm still a Reds fan. I'm going to try and sneak down to Tampa
next spring to watch them. I'm working on raising the money
for that now. I'm going on Amtrak. That's a whole different
crowd."

The soft drink guy is in convulsions. I press on with the interview before he can fumble the Faygo. Are you related to the
bank, I ask Winters.

"Used to be," he says, "but they lost that in the Depression.
That's when they gave my roller skates away."

The soft drink guy is semi-hysterical now. If Winters goes
into his Maudie Frickert stuff they're going to have to carry him

out in a doggy bag. I decide there is time for maybe one more question before he topples into his Tab.

Don't you ever get tired of being "on," I ask Winters. It's got to be tough to keep joking all the time.

"I don't do jokes, I do reality. Say, you paying me for this interview? No? Too bad. Anyway, the guy that just got in, he's kind of funny. I've stopped eating Skippy, but that's just for awhile. We should have gone through Atlanta twice."

The soft drink guy obviously is a Republican, because he is frantic with laughter now and in danger of swooning into the 7-Up.

I thank Jonathan Winters for his time and he tells me to be sure to tell all the guys in Dayton he says hello and to go to his bank because it beats Third National.

I promise to do that and I walk back to my seat in the press box. My suspicions have been confirmed. I have not wound up with material for a funny column.

The soft drink guy seemed to be amused, though.

3 The Woman Who Promised to Love, Honor, and Wash My Blue Flannel Pajamas

One day I talked to an Erma Bombeck fan who commented:
"I love to read her columns, because they reassure me that the things that happen around my house are normal."

I know what she means. I love to read Erma Bombeck's columns, too. But I still don't believe the things that happen around my house are normal.

Baby 1, D.L. O

Mar. 30, 1976

Quite some time ago I discovered that the best way to handle a baby is with a zone defense.

Here's how it works:

You station a mother in the kitchen, an older sister in the family room, an older brother upstairs. This does leave certain "seams" in your defense, such as the bathroom and the hall closet. But basically it's a pretty good setup because, when the kid becomes offensive, help is always nearby.

Last Thursday night my defense broke down.

The mother had a class to attend. The older sister went to a 4-H meeting. The older brother came down with a sudden attack of homework.

Suddenly I found myself in a man-to-man situation. One-on-one with the kid for the first time in his seven-month career.

"Don't worry," I was assured by the woman who had promised me that if I agreed to this one last bundle of joy, I would never have to so much as change a diaper. "He won't be any trouble at all."

And, for the first few minutes after she walks out the door, laughing her head off, she is right. The kid seems content, chewing on the coffee table and making funny little grunting sounds.

"Is his face usually that red?" I ask the 8-year-old, who has taken a break from the homework that he started five, long minutes ago.

"Couple times a day," he says.

Soon I figure out why the kid is making those funny little grunting sounds. It is as plain as the nose on my face. Either that, or the neighbor's septic tank is broken again.

"Better get me a washcloth," I tell the 8-year-old.

While he goes for the washcloth, I find a Pamper, pry the kid's mouth off the coffee table and lay him down on the family room floor.

The first half of the operation takes exactly 26 seconds. I know it is exactly 26 seconds, because that's as long as I can hold my breath.

After the old business is disposed of, I reach behind me for a new Pamper. When I turn around, the kid is gone. As he heads north, I catch a glimpse of his southern portion.

"Come back here," I yell, "we're not done yet."

If the kid hears me, he shows no signs of it as he crawls past the kitchen table and heads for the dining room. Being at an age where getting up off the floor is more trouble than it's worth, I decide to beat him at his own game. I crawl after him.

He has a half-room start on me, not to mention better acceleration. But I have him on experience and staying power. I catch him before he makes it to the stove and drag him back into the family room.

Apparently winded by the chase, the kid stays still as I apply the Pamper. But as I reach for his pants, he makes his move. This time I catch him before he makes the kitchen table. Back to the family room.

I roll him over on his back, holding one leg securely as I try to slip a pants leg over the other one. This is when I discover that it takes two hands to slide a pants leg over a kicking foot.

I let go of his other leg. He rolls over and starts to crawl again.

It is obvious that a new tactic is called for. I decide to dress him on the crawl. My only other alternative is to grow another hand. I crawl after him again, struggling to slide the pants on while we move.

The battle rages through the kitchen, across the dining room, into the living room. It is like trying to put pants on an alligator.

Just this side of the television I experience the thrill of victory. The pants are on him.

"That was great, Dad," the 8-year-old says. "But how come you put his pants on backwards?"

"Shut up and bring me my clipboard. I've got to figure out a new defense."

You Won't Have Any Trouble, She Said

Apr. 1, 1976

No special equipment is required to feed a 7-month-old kid. All it takes is a spoon, a dish, a washcloth and hands that are quick enough to slip mashed potatoes through an electric fan.

As I prepare to do battle across the high chair with the kid for the first time, all of these materials are present. I have the spoon, the dish and the washcloth.

Unfortunately, it is the kid who has the hands that are quick enough to slip mashed potatoes through an electric fan.

"You won't have any trouble feeding him," I have been reassured by the woman who promised that if I agreed to this one last bundle of joy, I would never have to so much as open a jar of strained apricots. "He has a good appetite."

I can't argue with that. In the half hour since she has left me alone with him, the kid already has eaten half a box of Posh Puffs, the contents of two ashtrays and the first 11 pages of the *Dayton Daily Whatchamacallit.* Serious illness was prevented because I stopped him before he got to the editorial pages.

Still, I feel a certain measure of unease as I prepare my opening move. She knows a grown man shouldn't have any trouble feeding a cute, little baby. And I know a grown man shouldn't have any trouble feeding a cute, little baby. But does the cute little baby know it?

The kid's food has been prepared in advance and rests in blobs in one of those three-section warming dishes. The menu consists of one section of green stuff and two sections of brown stuff with orange and white things in it. I try not to look at it.

The first few spoonsful of green stuff are greeted with open mouth. Whatever it is, he obviously likes it, because less than half is coming back out.

The brown stuff with the orange and white things in it is a different matter. With a right cross that Muhammad Ali only wishes he had, the kid sends the first spoonful sailing across the room. I hold his hands down and try again. His mouth snaps shut.

This obviously calls for the Stewart speed-spooning gambit.

In the Stewart speed-spooning gambit, you hide the ammunition behind your back, employ some kind of ruse to get the kid to open his mouth, then whip the stuff in there before he knows what's happening.

I hide a spoonful of the stuff behind my back. I give the kid my Steve Kirk routine, the one where I mess up my hair and go "AH-cha-cha-cha." The kid opens his mouth to laugh. With a lightning-fast move, I whip the spoon forward.

After I have cleaned the brown stuff out of the kid's ear, I decide to stick to the green stuff from now on.

I feed him green stuff until he indicates he has had enough. He indicates he has had enough by spitting the final spoonful of green stuff on my shirt.

I clean the green stuff off my shirt, the floor, the table, the high chair, the window and the telephone. I leave the green stuff on the wall. It looks nice against the yellow stuff he had for lunch. I give the brown stuff with the orange and white things to the dog. This is known as deep-sixing the evidence.

Soon it is time to get the kid ready for bed, using the bed-clothes that have been left for me in a pile on top of the television. The pile consists of a diaper, a Pamper, two pairs of rubber pants, an undershirt, an overshirt and an item known as a sleeper bag.

By the time I have put all this stuff on him, it is unclear to me whether I have prepared the kid for bed or for a winter on the Russian front.

But, finally, he is in bed.

At 10 o'clock the woman who is always telling me how rewarding it is for a father to spend some time alone with his children comes home.

"Did you have any trouble with him?" she asks.

"Trouble? What do you mean, trouble? How much trouble can a 7-month-old baby be?"

The Great Stork Race—in Real Life

July 8, 1975

The trouble with real life is that it's hardly ever like the movies.

Take the great stork race scene, for instance.

You know how that one goes. In the middle of the night she says, "George, I think it's time." Whereupon George leaps from the bed, knocks over a lamp, stumbles around in the dark

trying to get his pants on, falls down the stairs and sprints to
the garage with his shoes untied.

He throws her suitcase into the back seat, stammers "D-d-
don't worry, d-d-dear, we'll get you there in time," and
screeches out of the driveway. A few seconds later he returns
and gets her into the car, too.

At the hospital, where they have nothing to do but handle
this one delivery, he paces and puffs, paces and puffs. Fifteen
minutes and four packs later, a nurse and a doctor appear at the
door of the waiting room. The nurse is holding something wrap-
ped in a thick, white blanket. The doctor, dressed in a surgical
gown that is snow-white, crisply pressed and tailored by Brooks
Brothers, says, "Congratulations, George, it's a boy."

George pump the doctor's hands, jumps up and clicks his
heels and runs out of the hospital shouting, "Have a boy, it's a
cigar."

Somehow, we keep losing that script.

Like last Saturday.

It is 1 a.m. and the *Midnight Special* is starting to shine its
ever-lovin' light on us.

The woman who keeps telling me that she is never going to
go through this again, says, "I'm not sure, but I think this may
be the night."

"You gotta be kidding," I say. "Frankie Valli is going to sing
Rag Doll tonight. I've been looking forward to this all week."

It is 3 a.m. Frankie Valli has sung *Rag Doll*. *King of the
Khyber Rifles* stinks on Channel 2. Channel 5 is showing reruns
of *Peyton Place.* We decide we might as well go to the hospital.

It is 3:30 a.m. A lady meets us at the entrance of the Miami
Valley Hospital maternity ward and leads us to an elevator. The
doctor is waiting on the elevator. His shoes are untied. I feel
guilty about getting him out of bed. I wonder if he will feel guilty about sending me the bill.

The elevator deposits us on the fifth floor, where the
woman who keeps telling me she is never going to go through
this again is led away. The doctor heads for the bed he uses at
the hospital. The next time I see him he will be dressed in a

surgical gown that is moldy-green, freshly wrinkled and tailored by Columbo.

I am returned to the first floor and told to report to the admitting office, which is conveniently located four miles from the maternity entrance. At the admitting office a lady asks me the pertinent questions: Name, address, phone number, last night's Reds' score. I correctly answer two out of four.

I sign a form that says I am responsible for all the bills. It says nothing about repossession in the event of a default. Four miles and an elevator ride later I am back on the fifth floor.

It is 4 a.m. I am told to step into a waiting room. The room is empty except for three chairs, two paintings and a sign warning that it is illegal in this state to burn down a hospital due to careless smoking.

It is 4:20 a.m. The woman who says she is never going to go through this again joins me in the waiting room. She appears fresh and cheerful. But then, why shouldn't she? She isn't the one who just walked eight miles.

It is 5 a.m. A pleasant nurse named Fran comes along to check on the woman who says she's never going to go through this again. Fran has a question for me, too. What time is the Reds' games tonight? I am starting to feel like Marty Brennaman.

It is 5:35 a.m. Fran tells the woman who says she is never going to go through this again that she is "at 8." They both nod knowingly. Apparently being "at 8" is important, sort of like being over .300. I am told to go back to the first floor and wait.

It is 7 a.m. I am told to go back up to the fifth floor. There I am directed to a room. Inside the room is the woman who says she is never going to go through this again. She is holding something in a thin, faded blanket. It is red-faced, with puffy eyes, a swollen lip and a flattened nose. It looks like Rocky Graziano near the end of his career.

Obviously 22-minute-old Jamie Alan Stewart is not all that impressed with his first look at me, either. He begins to cry.

I didn't expect that. Somehow I figured the first thing he'd do when he saw me was ask who was pitching for the Reds tonight.

How I Still Missed the Big Game

Nov. 30, 1976

I always figured that football games were what being a father was all about.

Throughout the diaper years, the runny nose years, the crayons in the toilet years, the thought of football games sustained me. Someday, I would tell myself as I rolled up my sleeve and groped in the cold water, he will be big enough to take to a football game.

And the thought of us together at the game, me and my boy, would make it all worthwhile.

Sunday it finally happened. Sunday I took the 9-year-old to his first football game.

And not just any game. It is the Bengals-Steelers game, the biggest game of the year according to the advance notices. (Now, I understand, the biggest game of the year is next Monday's Bengals-Raiders game. That's the secret of pro football's success. It has an inexhaustible supply of biggest games of the year.)

Before we can leave for the biggest game of the year, however, we have to dress for it.

I dig out a pair of wool trousers, a bulky sweater, a turtleneck sweater, two pairs of sweat sox and fur-lined boots. The woman who promised to love, honor and never put my shirts in the underwear drawer, digs out my flannel pajama bottoms, the ones with the blue lions on them.

"What's this?" I ask, holding up the pajama bottoms.

"Flannel pajama bottoms with blue lions on them," she says.

"Very cute. But what am I supposed to do with them?"

"Wear them under your trousers."

"Do I have to?"

"Yes, because if you don't wear your pajama bottoms under your trousers, your son won't wear his pajama bottoms under his trousers. And he'll wind up catching a cold which will last all winter and he'll miss a lot of classes and fail fourth grade and probably drop out of school and wind up unemployable and have to resort to a life of crime and wind up in the pen by the age of 23."

"A simple yes or no would have been sufficient."

With our pajama bottoms under our trousers, we arrive at Riverfront Stadium 20 minutes before game time. I point out to the 9-year-old that it is a long way from our seats to the nearest restroom and he'd better go now before we sit down.

"I don't have to," he says.

"Are you sure?"

"Yep."

"Positive?"

"Yep."

So we skip the bathroom and go to our seats. The National Anthem is sung. The players are introduced. The Bengals kick off. The kid has to go to the bathroom.

We get back to our seats just in time for a television timeout.

"What did we miss?" I ask the guy next to me.

"A good run by Archie Griffin, a pretty pass to Trumpy and a terrific series by the Bengals' defense."

The game resumes. After a few mintues, the 9-year-old tugs at my sleeve.

"Can I have something to drink?"

I am prepared for this. I have brought along a Thermos of hot chocolate so I won't have to stand in the long lines at the concession stand and miss all the good plays. I look under the seat for the Thermos. While I am looking, the crowd roars.

"What happened?" I ask the guy next to me.

"Bengals kicked a field goal."

I pour the kid's hot chocolate. I sort of wish I had seen that field goal. But, what the heck. It's not like that's the only time the Bengals are going to score today.

It's the third quarter and snow coats the field. The 9-year-old tugs at my sleeve.

"I'm cold."

I turn in my seat to tighten up the hood of his jacket. While I am tightening, the crowd roars.

"What happened?" I ask the guy next to me.

"Franco Harris just scored for Pittsburgh."

I finish tightening the kid's hood. I sure wish I had seen that touchdown, which, it turns out, is the game-winner. But, what the heck. You see one winning touchdown in the biggest game of the year, you've seen them all.

The game ends. The trip home over icy, congested roads takes just four hours. Visibility is poor and a few times I am concerned about getting lost. It is a possibility that is too frightening to think about. I shudder at the thought of the police bulletin:

". . . when last seen, he was wearing wool trousers, a bulky sweater, a turtleneck sweater, two pairs of sweat sox, fur-lined boots and . . . heh, heh, pajama bottoms with . . . ha- ha-ha . . . blue . . . ho-ho-har . . . lions on them."

One Good Reason Not to Buy a Convertible

Sept. 14, 1976

Being an intuitive husband, I was quick to sense that my decision a few weeks ago to buy a convertible did not thrill the woman who had promised to love, honor and help me avoid the chuckholes of life.

It was nothing definite, you understand. Just something in the tone of her voice when she said: "Boy, the older you get, the dumber you get."

I mean, you live with a woman long enough and you start tuning in to the little nuances.

"Give me one good reason why I shouldn't buy a convertible," I demanded.

"They're not safe, they're cold in the winter, they leak when it rains, they rattle when you hit a bump, some vandal will probably cut the top to shreds and the rear window always gets so scratched up that you can't see out of it after about a month."

"I said give me ONE good reason. Anyway, you know you're exaggerating."

"Oh, really? What about the last convertible you bought?"

"Well, what about it?"

"Remember how cold it always was driving that thing in the winter?'

"Cold? It wasn't cold. That car had a terrific heater."

"Big deal. So our feet sweated while frost was forming on our noses. And how about the way it leaked everytime it rained?"

"It didn't leak that much," I protested.

"Then how come the standard equipment included a snorkel?"

As conversations around our house sometimes do, this one ended in pitiful sobbing and a torrent of tears. But eventually she relented and agreed that I could buy a convertible. So I dried my eyes and rushed down to the convertible car place.

So as not to be guilty of free advertising, I won't say what kind of car I bought. Let's just use the initials: M.G.

Besides, I'm not really sure what M.G. stands for.

The salesman, who was a veritable fountain of information on such matters as cubic inches, rear axle ratios and torque conversions, gave me a blank stare when I asked him about it.

"Nobody ever asked me that one before," he said. "Let me check with the sales manager."

The sales manager, who knew all about F.O.B., P.O.E. and A.P.R., likewise did not have the answer. But he said he would check with his boss.

His boss suggested that I buy a Triumph.

(Later I was told that M.G. stands for Miller's Garage, in recognition of the place where the first M.G. was put together. If this is true, it is easy to understand why they use the initials. Like, who wants to drive to the country club in his Miller's Garage?)

In any event, I bought the M.G., complete with wire wheels, AM-FM radio, anti-roll bar, luggage rack, tonneau cover and payments that will keep me eating macaroni and cheese for the next 36 months.

For the first week I drove happily around town, top down, with the blue sky up above, the wind in my hair, the suspended particulate matter in my eyes. Not even an unfortunate decision to pass a truck whose driver chewed tobacco could diminish my enthusiasm.

On the eighth day it rained, a fact brought to my attention

in this windowless office by a phone call from an anonymous tipster.

"Now you're in for it, dummy," she said. "It's raining outside and you left your top down. You're going to have to tread water on your way home."

"For your information," I retorted, "the car will hardly be wet at all, because I parked it under a tree on Fourth Street."

"A tree? What kind of tree?"

"How do I know what kind of tree? It's just a regular tree, with branches and leaves and twigs and birds."

There was a pause.

"You parked your car with the top down under a tree with birds in it?" she said, finally.

"Yeah."

There was another pause. Then there was laughter.

"Like I said, the older you get . . ."

Those Old Piano Roll Blues

Dec. 16, 1976

It's not that I have anything against pianos.

In their place, pianos are wonderful things. Their place includes Carnegie Hall, Archie Bunker's living room and Emmert Royer's commercials.

Their place does not include a house so crowded already that O.J. Simpson could not get through it without being tackled by a coffee table.

Which is what I try to point out to the woman who promised to love, honor and keep the exits clear when she mentions that Jerry and Lois have an extra piano in their basement that they'd be willing to give us. (Jerry and Lois are the only people I ever heard of with two pianos. Except for Ferrante and Teicher).

"We can put it in our basement," she replies when I point out that if we get a piano we're going to have to move the couch into the kitchen.

"But, I'm going to put my pool table in the basement."

"You don't have a pool table."

"But I will one of these days and there's not enough room

in that basement for a piano and a pool table. So you can just forget about the piano. You can tell Jerry and Lois 'Thanks, but no thanks' and then put it out of your mind. We are absolutely not going to get a piano and I don't want to hear anymore about it. That's my final word."

The piano arrived last Wednesday.

It is one of those old upright models. It weighs a little more than the Pittsburgh Steelers and it is a little wider than Rhode Island.

Most of all, it is five inches taller than the basement stairwell.

"The best way to get it down there," says one of the deliverymen after measuring all the angles, "is to take five inches off the ceiling. Or, you could remove the bottom four steps."

I give the deliverymen their $45 for bringing our free piano and show them out before one of them suggests chopping a hole in the kitchen floor or maybe jacking up the house and sliding the piano underneath.

Then we are alone. Me, the woman who promised to love, honor and tickle my ivories, and a free piano that so far has cost me $45 and at this moment is sitting in the family room obscuring the $1,000 fireplace.

"I sort of like it there," she says. "Can't you just picture us on Christmas Eve, gathered around the piano, singing carols, with a fire going in the fireplace?"

"I could, except that nobody in our family knows how to play the piano."

"Quit being such a nit-picker and help me move the couch into the kitchen."

So now the piano is in the family room, the couch is in the kitchen, the pool table is in my imagination and the 4-year-old is banging his Evel Knievel Stunt Cycle on the white keys at 7:30 in the morning.

But if you happen to be in the neighborhood on Christmas Eve, look us up. We'll be the ones gathered around the piano. In the family room. Singing "Chopsticks."

How Green My Valley, How High the Grass

May 22, 1976

The-grass-is-so-high-and-I'm-so-low-and-I-sure-wish-I-was-back-living-in-an-apartment-baby blues:

Long ago, when I was much younger and nearly as smart as I thought I was, we lived in an apartment. Two bedrooms, bath and a half, wall-to-wall carpet and a tiny patch of grass in the back that a little man came around once a week to cut.

But then the family began to grow and I was informed by the woman who had promised never to hang her nylons on the shower head that it was time to move.

"The kids need more room," she said.

"Okay, let's rent a bigger apartment."

"No. We've got to buy a house," she said.

"I absolutely refuse to buy a house. Buying a house is nothing but trouble. We're not going to buy a house and that's my final word on the subject."

The house we bought had three bedrooms, wall-to-wall ceilings and a quarter-acre of grass. But with a few curtains and a little paint I suddenly was king of my own castle and feeling pretty good about it all.

It was about two weeks after we moved in that the queen of the castle said, "Did you happen to notice how tall the grass is getting?"

"Yeah, I noticed that. Wonder where that little man is?"

"Houses don't have little men," she said. "You have to cut it yourself."

"I knew there was a catch. But, the thing is, we don't have a lawn mower. Anyway, I don't like the looks of those things. They're noisy and smelly and the neighbors always seem to be having troubles with theirs."

"Well, you better do something. The kids are getting grass stains on their shirts."

"Well, they shouldn't be lying in the grass."

"They're not."

Just in time we were rescued by the man next door.

"I've got this old mower in my garage that you can have,"

he offered. "I don't need it, but I never got around to throwing it out."

And he hauls a rusty old mower out of his garage, the kind that makes no noise and no fumes, because it has no engine.

Saturday morning, when all the neighbors are out with their power mowers, I take my push mower out of the garage and start to push. Before I have finished the front, most of the kids on the block have assembled on the sidewalk to watch.

"What's that you're pushing, mister?"

"How come it's so quiet?"

"Who stealed your engine?"

"Hey, mister, how come you're sweating so much?"

The old push mower lasted for about a month. Well, actually, it lasted longer than that. For all I know, it may still be working. But I only lasted for a month.

"That's just too darned much work," I said to the woman who had promised to always be at my side as I battled the crabgrass of life. "We've just got to get a power mower."

"Boy, men today are really soft," she sneered, with a disdainful twist of the dial on her automatic dishwasher.

So I got a used electric mower for $50 and it was simple and quiet and didn't make any fumes. And it would have been perfect, except that when you needed to cut the far corner of the yard you had to borrow an extension cord from the toaster.

For two years I used that electric mower, while the kids learned to eat their eggs with plain bread.

But still the family continued its mysterious growth and once again I was informed that it was time to move.

"The kids need more room," she said.

"Well, if you think we're going to buy a new house, you can just forget it. We don't need it, we can't afford it and we're not going to get it. That's final."

Our new house had four bedrooms, wall-to-wall water under the basement and a half-acre of grass.

And on the first day I went out to mow I learned that if you borrowed the extension cord from the toaster and also the one from the blender, you could still only reach about half the yard.

So I bought me a power mower, the kind with the noise

and the fumes and the mechanical problems, for $130. I don't want to say what brand it is, but it has a picture of a dog on the front, which probably should have been a tip-off.

After two and a half years, the mower with the picture of the dog on the front broke down this spring and I was informed by a neighbor who knows about such things that it was beyond repair.

"What you need," he said, "is a rider mower. You can get a good one for five, six hundred bucks. Get yourself one of those babies and your lawn mowing problems will be solved."

Maybe. But somehow I don't think that's the answer. Somehow I don't think my lawn mowing problems will ever be solved. Not unless that little man comes back.

Mower Trouble—and Where Is Mary Anne?

July 1, 1976

The - grass - is - getting - higher - and - I'm - getting - lower - and - I - sure - do - wish - I - could - cover - the - whole - mess - with - Astroturf - mama - blues, Part II.

In Part I, you may recall, the grass was knee high, the mower had just received last rites, and I was wondering whatever happened to the little man who used to come around and mow the lawn at the apartment where we used to live.

That was more than a month ago, and few things have changed since then. Except that now the grass is somewhat higher and the woman who promised to love, honor and help me fight chickweed is becoming surly.

"You planning on cutting the grass anytime this summer?" she says one day.

"Why do you ask?"

"The neighbors are getting sort of upset."

"Which neighbors?"

"The ones behind us."

"I didn't know we had neighbors behind us."

"That's just the point."

"Well, OK. I'll go next door and borrow Bob and Mary Anne's rider mower."

"Bob and Mary Anne moved two weeks ago."

"They did? Are you sure?"

"Positive. I saw the top of their moving van."

"You didn't happen to notice if they took their mower with them?"

"They took everything but their dog."

"Why didn't they take their dog?"

"They haven't been able to find him since he wandered into our backyard three weeks ago."

"All right, all right. I'll go buy a mower."

So I head for a department store downtown, the identity of which I won't reveal. Let's just say its last name is Roebuck. I select this particular store for two reasons. First, because it advertises a rider mower for just $300. Second, because it is the only store in town that doesn't laugh when it checks our credit rating.

"I'd like to see the $300 rider mower," I tell the sales clerk.

"Certainly sir," he says. "It's right here. May I point out some of its features for you?"

He points out some of its features. Among its top features are four tires and pretty green paint.

"To be honest with you," the clerk admits, "for $300 you can't expect too much. For one thing, adjusting the blade height is a little complicated."

"How complicated?"

"Well . . . I don't suppose you have a degree from MIT?"

"I don't think this mower is exactly what I'm looking for," I say.

"In that case, I just happen to have a model over here that might interest you."

Whenever salesmen start a sentence with, "I just happen to have . . ." I tend to get nervous. But the second mower turns out to be just what I am looking for. It has four tires and pretty red paint. It is not new, but the salesman assures me the previous owner was a little old man who drove it only on Sundays. And it comes with a full warranty.

On a Thursday afternoon, the mower is delivered. As it is being taken off the truck, a crowd gathers. The people who live behind us show up. They have always wondered what color our house is, they say. Bob and Mary Anne show up all the way from Chicago. They have always wondered what happened to their dog, they say.

I start up my new mower. I put it in gear. I push the "blade engage" lever and begin to mow. My new mower does everything you could want a mower to do. Except, maybe, cut the grass.

"How come it's not cutting the grass?" I ask Bob.

We turn the mower over. Bob checks it out.

"You've got a broken belt," he says.

I call the store and tell them about my broken belt.

"How long have you had the mower?" the man at the store asks.

"About 25 minutes."

"In that case, your warranty may still be in effect. Let me check."

A few minutes later he returns to the phone.

"Good news, sir. There's still some time left on your warranty. We'll get somebody out there right away to fix it."

That was two weeks ago. The mower still isn't fixed. The grass is still growing. What's worse, Bob is staying at our house. He says he won't leave until he finds Mary Anne.

Don't Forget To Turn Off The Water

Jan. 6, 1977

Fixing a leaky faucet is no big hassle. Some of the happiest weeks of my life have been spent fixing leaky faucets. In the last two months alone I've fixed the one in the downstairs bathroom five times.

The last time was this past Sunday, just after the woman who promised to love, honor and never nag about household repairs brings up the subject in her own subtle way.

"You ever going to fix that crummy faucet?" she says.

"You promised never to nag about household repairs, remember?"

"You're absolutely right. I'm wrong. I apologize. I have no right whatsoever to mention something like that on your day off. I know you work hard all week, typing your fingers to the bone, and you need your rest on the weekends. It is really lousy of me to bother you about a mere leaky faucet, even though it is probably costing us a hundred bucks extra on our water bill every three months. But don't worry about the extra money, because I can always cut corners by watering down the baby's milk or maybe I could take in washing or scrub floors for the rich people in Oakwood, so you just sit there and . . ."

"All right, all right, I'll fix the damn faucet."

So I get my tools and I go to work.

To fix the faucet in the downstairs bathroom, the first thing you have to do is remove the medicine chest so you can get to it. I've never been able to figure out why it is that the medicine chest hangs $2\frac{1}{2}$ inches over the faucet. I even called the architect who designed our house to ask him about it several years ago. But he was in Detroit at the time. Working on the Corvair.

After I have removed the medicine chest, I unscrew the faucet handle and start to untighten the faucet assembly. After I have retightened the faucet assembly and mopped the bathroom floor, I go down to the basement and turn off the water.

Back upstairs, I untighten the faucet assembly again and take it out. I also take out a little gold thing that has threads on the bottom and a hexagonal hole on top. This is the part that is causing the leak.

So I drive to the He-Man Hardware Store (not its real name), which is not one of my favorite places in the whole world.

The reason it is not one of my favorite places in the whole world is because whenever I walk in there I always feel like the sissy from the East walking into the Long Branch Saloon. Like, there are always guys standing around with splinters in their fingers and steel rules on their belts and they're saying words like "joist" and "ratchet wrench" and "router bit" and other words I don't understand.

Usually I wind up walking out without buying anything, because if I want something I never know what to call it and even if I know what to call it I never know what size I need.

This time, however, I have come prepared. I have brought the entire faucet assembly with me, including the little gold thing. They're not going to intimidate me this time.

I walk up to the counter boldly, just like the guy in the beer commercial.

"Lemme have one of these," I say, flipping the little gold thing on the counter in front of the salesman.

"Seat," he says.

"Nope, I'll stand."

"That's what it's called. A faucet seat."

"Oh, sure. I knew that."

"What kind of sink is this out of?" he asks.

"Bathroom."

"Yeah, but what's the manufacturer's name?"

Suddenly my confidence is destroyed. My ratchet is wrenched. My router is bit. I have absolutely no idea what kind of sink it is.

Eventually, however, the salesman determines what kind of faucet seat is called for. It is a 33/64ths-27. I should have known that.

Back home, I put in the 33/64ths-27 faucet seat. I tighten the faucet assembly. I screw on the faucet handle. I rehang the medicine chest. I turn on the water downstairs. I turn on the faucet upstairs. The faucet works perfectly.

Unfortunately, it leaks. I have wasted the entire afternoon.

On the other hand, I'll have something to do next Sunday.

Mr. Build-It Strikes Again

Apr. 14, 1977

I would, undoubtedly, be a better father today if I had taken more industrial arts courses in high school.

As it was, I took just one semester of shop, during which I struggled to complete the two required projects—a garden trowel and a lamp. I received a "C" in the course, mostly because the instructor couldn't tell which was the lamp.

All of which did little to prepare me for the Pinewood Derby, which is coming up again this month.

The Pinewood Derby is an annual event staged by the Cub Scouts, one of whom lives in our house.

The idea of the Pinewood Derby is for the Scout and his dad to build a little model race car from a block of wood. After the cars are built, they are raced down an elevated track to determine which Scout's dad has the best power tools.

My introduction to the Pinewood Derby came two years ago, when our Cub Scout came home with a small brown paper bag.

"What's in the small brown paper bag?" I ask, ever-alert for opportunities to prove that I am a vitally interested parent, concerned with the problems, achievements and aspirations of my children.

"Race car," he says.

"Great. Let's have a look at it."

He opens the small brown paper bag and spreads the contents out on the kitchen table. There is a block of wood, two smaller pieces of wood, four nails and four plastic wheels.

"Where's the race car?" I ask.

"That's it," he says. "All we have to do is carve the wood until it looks like this." He holds up a picture of a Jaguar XKE. It doesn't look anything like a block of wood.

I start to explain to him about the garden trowel and the

lamp. I try to point out to him that the chances of me making a race car out of that block of wood are comparable to the chances of me luring Farrah Fawcett away from Lee Majors.

"Don't worry, dad," he interrupts. "I'll do the hard parts."

With that, he takes the block of wood and disappears into the basement.

For more than an hour I hear nothing from him. Finally, I go down to investigate.

The block of wood still looks like a block of wood. I'm not sure where the Pinewood Derby people get the materials, but I suspect it is from the petrified forest. In more than an hour, the only thing he has been able to whittle is a chunk out of the Ping-Pong table.

I decide that I had better take over. After all, whittling is dangerous for a 7-year-old kid. The knife is sharp and he might cut himself.

It takes me only three hours to chip the block of wood into something reminiscent of an auto body. I could have done it faster, but it took almost half an hour to find the Band-Aids.

With the whittling finished, the rest is easy. A little paint here, a wheel there and the car is finished. It is not a Jaguar XKE exactly, but at least he will have something to enter in the competition.

Semi-proudly, I carry it upstairs.

The Cub Scout is in bed, but the woman who promised to love, honor and keep her hands off my router bits is in the living room.

"Look what I made," I say.

"Oh good," she says. "We needed a garden trowel."

Click, Click . . . Abort One Christmas Plan

Dec. 27, 1975

I know, I know, it's not really possible to defeat Christmas. But this year I had fully expected to fight it to a draw. Because this year I approached it scientifically, with a master plan.

The plan became operative two weeks ago, when I accompanied the woman who had promised to love, honor and do all the Christmas shopping to the department store. Not that she needed help. Anybody whose credit cards are wrinkled has to be considered a veteran.

Mainly I go along to make sure she doesn't buy any of those easy-to-assemble numbers, the ones that require only a few simple tools and a master's degree from MIT.

As I deftly steer her away from the 10-speed English racers that take only a few minutes to put together, I move into Part B.

"Don't forget to buy them some active toys," I suggest. "If it's under 70 degrees on Christmas Day, you know they won't go outside. So get them some stuff that will keep them busy running around in the basement. That way they'll burn up a lot of energy and be ready for bed by 7:30."

Obviously impressed by the simple beauty of the plan, she purchases a plastic bowling game that will not harm the furniture, an indoor basketball set that will hang on any standard door and a Ping-Pong kit for the second-hand table that has stood in the basement for six months without benefit of net.

Christmas Eve goes according to plan. It is the first in memory that does not include fastening Part C to Part D with wing nut G.

Christmas morning also proceeds smoothly and an entire family room full of presents is torn open in 15 minutes, bettering last year's time of 17:43.09.

The plan is working so perfectly that there is even time to watch *Miracle on 34th Street*.

At 11 a.m., it is time to swing into Part C.

"I think I'll go down to the basement and put up the Ping-Pong net," I announce. In 30 seconds the net is up and I am engaged in a brisk game with the 11-year-old. Well, not brisk, exactly. A brisk game goes click-click-click. Ours went click—"I'll get it"—click—"I think it's under the washing machine"—click—"Well, let's use the other ball."

But after an hour or so, the 11-year-old says that she is getting tired. Suppressing a triumphant smile, I start up the stairs. On the third step, I am intercepted by the 8-year-old, who wants to play the indoor basketball game.

"Sure," I say, "I'll just hang it on a door and we'll play."

It is at this point that the master plan displays its first flaw.

There are no doors in the basement.

But I improvise. It takes little more than an hour to drill the necessary holes into the basement wall, which is made of the hardest cement block known to man. It takes only a few simple tools to attach the hoop to the wall. As I fasten Part C to Part D with wing nut G, I experience a strange sensation. Deja vu, I think they call it.

The basketball game lasts half an hour before the 8-year-old says he is tired. I am starting to feel a little fatigued myself, but I am buoyed by the knowledge that the master plan is working perfectly.

Halfway up the stairs, I am confronted by the 3-year-old, who informs me that it is time to play the bowling game that will not damage the furniture.

The reason that the bowling game will not damage the furniture is that the pins are made of soft plastic. Soft plastic pins will not damage furniture. Soft plastic pins also will not stand up. At least, not all 10 of them at once. But, finally, after five minutes of coaxing, I get them standing. It takes him two seconds to knock them down.

"Set 'em up again, Dad," he demands. Five minutes later they are set up. Two seconds after that they are down again. The fun goes on for quite awhile before he says that he is tired.

Success. All three of them are worn out. The master plan has worked perfectly. I am a genius, albeit a tired one. I start up the stairs for a well-deserved rest. I am met by the 11-year-old.

"Let's play some more Ping-Pong," she says.
"But I thought you were tired."
"I was. But I'm not anymore. I rested up while you were playing basketball and bowling."

"Well, why don't you play with your brother?"
"Oh, he's resting so he can play some more basketball."

It's back to the basement for more Ping-Pong. And back to the drawing board for a new master plan.

A Little Yuletime Realism, Please

Dec. 28, 1976

In the Christmases of Hollywood and television commercials, there is a handsome daddy, a beautiful mommy, a little girl who is blonde and a little boy who has freckles.

On Christmas morning they float down the stairs together. The daddy is wearing tailored pajamas that have no wrinkles in them, which means that either he just put them on or he slept standing up. The mommy is wearing Dior's latest. The little girl who is blonde is cute as a button. The little boy who has freckles is cute as two buttons.

They gather around the 14-foot high tree to open their presents.

For the daddy there is a $1,000 watch. For the mommy there is a $1,000 diamond ring. The little girl who has blonde hair gets a dolly. The little boy who has freckles gets a train.

After they have stacked the boxes and folded the wrapping paper, the children say in unison: "Gosh, Mommy and Daddy, this was our best Christmas ever."

I hate that family.

I hope the daddy's watch gets ripped off by a mugger in the subway. I hope the mommy's diamond falls out of its setting and goes down the drain and the plumber has to be called and the bill is $126. I hope the little girl's dolly gets chewed up by the mean dog next door. I hope the little boy's train shorts out and he has to wait six months to get a new engine shipped from Hackensack, N.J.

Most of all I hope that whole crummy family gets stuck at our house Christmas morning and learns what it is really like.

What it is really like is that at 6:30 a.m. the little girl who has blonde hair is in our bedroom playing "You're A Grand Old Flag" on the kazoo that somebody was dumb enough to put in her stocking.

So we get out of bed, me and the woman who promised to love, honor and never again put a kazoo in anybody's stocking.

We lurch down the stairs together.

I am wearing my mix and match pajamas: Blue lion tops,

orange race car bottoms. She is wearing K-Mart's latest. There is a little girl who is blonde and a little boy who has freckles, but there is also another little boy who has chicken pox and a third little boy who needs to be changed.

We gather around the tree, the one that is in the corner this year so you can't see its bare sides, and we open the presents.

For the daddy there is a set of V-neck T-shirts, two pairs of dark blue socks, a plastic puzzle that he will never be able to get back together and a project made in Cub Scouts that is either a key chain or a pencil holder.

For the mommy there is a jump suit that is too small. On the other hand, she doesn't like the color.

For the little girl who is blonde there is a doll. There is also a 30-piece wardrobe (29 sweatshirts and a pair of pre-grubbied jeans), a record album, a coin collector's set, a pottery kit, a comb and brush set, a pound-and-a-half of costume jewelry and an electronic calculator which will enable her to add, subtract, multiply, divide and compute the theory of relativity. Unless there is a power failure.

For the little boy with the freckles, there is a mountain of toys that was delivered last week by Rike's. In a semi. His favorite is a junior magician set. Until he learns that he can't make his sister disappear.

For the little boy with the chicken pox, there is a mountain of toys delivered by two semis. His favorite is an SSP car that makes noise and throws off sparks and belongs to his brother.

The little boy who needs changing, being too young to know when he is getting the shaft, receives only a molehill of toys. His favorite is the box that the musical top comes in.

And then the last present has been torn open. The last fancy bow has been mashed into the rug. The last one-year warranty has been thrown into the fire.

And the children look up at the mommy and the daddy and they say in unison:

"Gosh, mommy and daddy, ain't there nuthin' else?"

Stick that in your script, Hollywood.

It's Not the Fall That Hurts So Bad

Jan. 22, 1976

VALLEY HI, Ohio — Sure, I fell down eight times during my first attempt at skiing last week.

But that's not what hurt.

I mean, I was prepared to fall down, because I had done a lot of studying in preparation for my debut last Saturday at Mad River Mountain. And among the things my research uncovered was that whenever you have skiing, you have falling down.

I knew a lot of things about skiing before I tried it. Like, I knew you should always replace your sitzmarks. And you should never finish your run on a different pair of skis than the ones you started with. And it is considered bad form in ski circles to ride the chair lift down a mountain.

Of course, there were some things about skiing I didn't know. For instance, I didn't know how to put the skis on, so the instructor had to do that for me, like a kindergarten teacher helping a kid put on his boots. That was sort of embarrassing.

But that's not what really hurt.

After the instructor, whose name is Dick Zinn, got the skis fastened he suggested that we take a few minutes to get used to the feel of them. Unless you have worn skis, it is difficult to imagine how they feel the first time you try to move in them. But try to picture having size eight feet and wearing size 14 shoes.

"OK," Dick Zinn said after awhile, "let's walk around a little bit before we try going down any hills."

"Fine," I said.

"Fine," said the woman who has been helping me go downhill for years. I probably should point out here that she is lovely but not very coordinated.

I took my first step on skis. Not too bad. I tried my second step. What the heck? The ski wouldn't move.

I glanced back over my shoulder, at the woman who is lovely, but not very coordinated.

"Uh, dear, you're standing on my ski."

"No dear, you're standing on your own ski."

"Oh . . . yeah."

But that's not what hurt, either.

When he was satisfied that we were able to walk well enough to be able to move out of the way of a medium-fast glacier, Dick Zinn announced that the next lesson was learning how to fall.

"Pay attention, dear," I said to the woman who is lovely, but not very coordinated, "you're going to need this."

"Learning to fall properly is very important," Dick Zinn commented. "The best place to fall is on the spot where God gave you a natural pillow.

"That's the one behind you," he added, taking note of the fact that God had seen fit to give me more than one natural pillow.

But that's not what hurt.

Dick Zinn, who is a Dayton native and a very good teacher, taught us a whole bunch of things after that.

He showed us how to bring the toes of the skis together in the event we wanted to stop in an area where there were no convenient trees. He explained how we should bend our knees, and lean forward and shift our weight and all that kind of stuff.

Then he said we were ready to try skiing.

After one last look at my unbroken limbs, I pushed off at the top of a hill that appeared to be just slightly steeper than Mt. Fuji. Instantly I knew that I was going to fall before I got halfway down. I was wrong. I fell before I got a third of the way down.

But that's not what hurt. I mean, yeah, it did hurt. But that's not what really hurt.

Lying there, sprawled and unable to regain my feet, I looked back up the hill to where the woman who is lovely, but not very coordinated, was starting her descent. Slowly she glided over the snow. Slowly she drew even with me. Slowly she went on past me, all the way to the bottom.

"That was very good," Dick Zinn shouted to her.

"Oh," he added, looking back to where I still lay on the snow, "you fell very nicely, too."

But that's not what hurt.

Again we tried it. Again I fell. Again the woman who is lovely, but not very coordinated, made it all the way to the bottom.

For two hours we skied. Push off. Bend your knees. Lean forward. Oops. After two hours I was covered with snow, especially on the pillows that God had given me.

Finally we decided that we had had enough. We retired to the lodge, to have a mug of mocha coffee and discuss skiing. To talk over the ups and downs of the day, you might say.

"You know," I said to the woman who is lovely, but not very coordinated, "falling down isn't all that bad. It's trying to get up again with those skis on that's really tough."

The woman who is lovely, but not very coordinated, looked at me over her mug of mocha coffee.

"I wouldn't know about that," she said, sweetly.

THAT'S what hurt.

Fools Schuss In

Jan. 18, 1977

It was my idea to go skiing last Saturday.

"Remember how it was last time?" I say to the woman

who promised to love, honor and cover my sitz marks. "The cold wind in our faces. The exhilaration of gliding over the snow. The invigorating exercise."

"You got so much energy, Jean Claude Killy, how about shoveling the driveway," she says.

"What? And risk a heart attack?"

So I give the kid up the street $3 to shovel the driveway and we hop in the car and drive to Mad River Mountain ski area near Bellefontaine.

Mad River Mountain is where I made my skiing debut last year. It is the place where I became an instant Alpine legend by falling down 23 times.

This year, however, I am determined not to spend the entire day in the bar.

When we arrive at the ski area, we go to the equipment rental counter, where young men are waiting to help us locate the proper equipment.

"What size shoe do you wear?" one of the young men asks.

"10½," I tell him. He digs out a pair of boots.

"And how much do you weigh?"

"Dressed or stripped?"

"Which way you planning on skiing?"

When we are properly equipped, we proceed to the area where the moguls are located. "Mogul" is an ancient Scandinavian word. It means, "practically flat area where only someone with absolutely no coordination could possibly fall down."

I fall down three times on the moguls. Then I put on my skis.

"This year," I announce to the woman who promised to love, honor and pick up the pieces, "I am going to try the beginner's slope."

While she heads for a phone to notify the Bellefontaine Rescue Unit, I head for the tow rope, which is the device that conveys you to the top of the beginner's slope.

"Tow rope" is an old Bavarian phrase. It means, "moving rope that tears your arms out of their sockets and gives your palms second degree burns the first time you grab it."

I am not aware of this as I head for the spot where the tow rope begins, however. I am too busy thinking about my impending debut on the beginner's slope and how I am determined not to fall coming down. How embarrassing it would be to fall coming down the beginner's slope, the gentle little hill that is used by small children and elderly persons and women who are great with child. There could be nothing more embarrassing than falling coming down the beginner's slope.

With these thoughts going through my mind, I grab the tow rope. I feel a tearing sensation in my shoulders. A burning sensation in my palms. And a hot flush on my cheeks. Because I have just learned that there is something more embarrassing than falling down the beginner's slope. Falling going UP the beginner's slope.

Eventually I master the intricacies of the tow rope and it drags me to the top of the beginner's slope.

At the top of the beginner's slope I become aware of a peculiar phenomenon: The hill that appeared so gentle and harmless from down below is, in reality, slightly steeper than Mt. Rainier. And the longer you stand there, the steeper it gets.

Before it has time to become Mt. Everest, I push off from the top of the hill.

And then I am skiing.

I am gliding over the glistening snow.

I am racing across the white slope.

I am hurtling down the frozen chasm.

I am about to break every bone in my body.

Unable to stop, I plunge down the hill out of control. As I plunge, a question flashes across my mind.

"Why are you doing this?"

Just before I wipe out, an answer flashes across my mind.

"Because you're stupid."

When the pain has passed, I unfasten the skis. I carry them back to the equipment rental counter. I head for the ski lodge bar.

"Ski lodge bar" is an old American phrase. It means, "area where anybody with a lick of sense would never leave in the first place."

The Rice Isn't All That Gets Fried

Sept. 11, 1976

The decision to do "something different" on our wedding anniversary this year was reached by means of a unanimous vote taken during my absence.

"What we're going to do," I was informed by the woman who promised to love, honor and always consult me before making any important decisions, "is stay home and cook a really fabulous meal together. Then we can have a romantic dinner with wine and candles instead of going out and wasting a lot of money at some restaurant."

"Don't I have anything to say about this?" I protested.

"Of course you do, dear. You can decide what kind of meal we'll cook."

A few days later I learned that I had decided we would cook a Chinese meal. Which came as something of a surprise to me, seeing as how I don't particularly like Chinese food.

On Monday night we go to the supermarket to purchase the ingredients for our anniversary dinner. The bill comes to $23.97. Ordinarily it wouldn't cost that much. It's just that we are fresh out of bamboo shoots, bean sprouts, pea pods and ginger root.

The store is out of sake (pronounced SAH-key). Instead, we substitute rose (pronounced ro-ZAY) and liebfraumilch (pronounced LEEB-frau-milch). We buy sufficient rose and liebfraumilch to guarantee a successful evening (pronounced BOMB-ed).

Tuesday night we prepare our gourmet Chinese anniversary dinner.

The first step is to divide the duties. She volunteers to chop up the ingredients for the almond chicken gai ding. I volunteer to test the liebfraumilch. By the time she has finished preparing the mushrooms, green onions and pea pods, I have finished testing the liebfraumilch.

She puts aside the mushrooms, onions and pea pods. They will be cooked later. I put aside the liebfraumilch bottle. It will be picked up by the garbage man tomorrow.

While she tests the rose, I set to work de-boning the chicken breasts. De-boning chicken breasts is a tricky business, even when the chicken is dead. But I soon establish a rhythm.

Slice a piece of chicken, throw it in the pot, toss the scraps to the dog, take a sip of cooking sherry. Slice another piece of chicken, throw it in the pot, toss the scraps to the dog, take two sips of cooking sherry. Slice a piece of chicken, throw it to the dog, toss the scraps in the pot, take three sips of cooking sherry. Slice a piece of scrap, throw the dog in the pot, toss the chicken on the floor and guzzle the cooking sherry.

Finally all the scraps are in the pot, the chicken is in the dog, the cooking sherry bottle is in the trash and it's time to fix the lion's head soup.

Despite what you might think, lion's head soup does not contain lions' heads. The main ingredients are celery, chicken broth, green onions, spinach, raw eggs and sherry. Put it all together and it reminds you a great deal of where the Great Miami flows under the Monument Street Bridge.

While the lion's head soup simmers, we make the shrimp fried rice. Shrimp fried rice consists of shrimp and rice. Fried.

Next we work on the egg rolls. Egg rolls consist of everything that's left over from the lion's head soup, stuffed into a special thin shell. If your local supermarket does not carry these special thin shells, shingles may be substituted.

After the egg rolls have been stuffed, we prepare the almond chicken gai ding. Almond chicken gai ding consists of almonds, chicken and gai. Ding is optional. Ideally, this should be cooked in an Oriental utensil known as a wok, but an electric fry pan made in Japan will do just as well.

Finally, everything is complete. The lion's head soup is finished. The egg rolls are finished. The shrimp fried rice is finished. The rose is finished. The cooking sherry is finished. It is 1:30 in the morning and we are in no shape to eat.

We leave the food on the table. The kids can have almond chicken gai ding for breakfast.

As we head up the stairs, she says, "That was fun. Let's do it again next year."

"Right. I know just what we can make."

"What's that?"

"Reservations at King Cole."

4 Weird? Whaddya Mean Weird?

Jim Murray, the popular sports columnist, says that asking him to select his favorite column is like asking him to decide "which of my children I like the best."

But if I had to pick out a favorite column of mine, it would be one of the ones in this chapter of fables, fantasies and outrageous puns.

I like fables and fantasies because, as Aesop knew, they can be used to make a point without getting you in trouble. When's the last time you heard of anybody getting sued for libel by a tortoise or a hare?

And I like outrageous puns because, whenever I hand one in, the city editor turns puce.

Children's Fare a Grimm Tale

Mar. 18, 1976

An elderly woman is crushed beneath a falling house.

Her sister shrivels to death.

A young girl is kidnaped, screaming, by weird creatures with wings on their backs.

A man in a scarecrow suit is brutally dismembered, his leg thrown "over there," his arm thrown "over here."

The *Wizard of Oz* was, the critics agreed, a refreshing change of pace from the usual violent fare with which television is destroying our children.

But television is not the only medium having trouble with sex and violence. Book publishers are having the same types of problems. If you don't believe me, let's go eavesdrop at Kinder and Garten, the children's book publishing company, where at this very moment an editor is interviewing an aspiring author.

★ ★ ★

"C'mon in and sit down, Mr. Grimm. You'll have to excuse me if I seem a little harried today. It's just that we've been getting a lot of flak this week from various parents' groups. They're raising hell about the sex and violence in some of our books.

"But, I'll tell ya, it's no picnic finding acceptable stories these days. You ought to see some of the stuff that writers have been submitting.

"Like this one, for instance. It's about a wolf that terrorizes three pigs and winds up getting scalded to death. Can you imagine what the PTAs would do to us if we came out with a book like that?

"And here's another one. A kid breaks into a neighbor's home, steals his goose and magic harp and then kills the guy by making him fall off a giant beanstalk.

"I tell you, Grimm, this stuff is brutal. Even the poetry they're sending in would curl your typewriter ribbon. Look at this one. It's a rhyme about a farmer's wife who mutilates three handicapped animals. Lord, what the SPCA wouldn't do to us if we came out with something like that.

"And the sex. You wouldn't believe it. Just the other day I get a manuscript about some guy named Georgie Porgie, who goes around assaulting young girls and making them hysterical.

"Oh, and here's a dilly. It's about a baby whose cradle is hung up in a tree. Right there you gotta wonder, right? I mean, why would anybody hang a baby's bed in a tree? But that's not the worst of it. After awhile the branch breaks and the kid falls out.

"Now, what kind of weirdo would think up a story like that? Believe me, Grimm, you get all kinds of sickies in this business.

"But enough of my problems. Why don't you tell me a little about this story of yours?"

"Well, Mr. Kinder, my story is about a young girl who is going to her grandmother's house."

"Good. Good. The family angle."

"Yes. But before she gets there, she is met by a wolf who . . ."

"Wait a minute. I told you, sex is out."

"Oh no, Mr. Kinder, it's nothing like that. The wolf merely wants the food she is carrying in her basket."

"Well, OK. We'll let that go for now."

"Thank you. As I was saying, the wolf attempts to talk the girl into giving him her basket. When she refuses, he takes a shortcut through the woods to the grandmother's house and eats the old lady."

"He does WHAT?"

"He eats the grandmother."

"Listen, Grimm, I thought I made all that clear. That kind of stuff just won't go these days. I mean, it would be bad enough if he stabbed her or maybe planted a bomb in her car. But EAT her? You gotta be kidding."

"Well, perhaps I can alter that a bit. Anyway, after he takes care of the grandmother, he waits for the girl. When she arrives he eats her, too. Then he falls asleep and a huntsman comes along and slits open the wolf's belly. The girl and her grandmother hop out, the huntsman fills the wolf's stomach with rocks and the wolf dies a painful death."

"Good lord, Grimm, you don't really expect me to consider

a story like that, do you? We'd have every parents' group in the country on our necks."

"Well, how about this one? A boy and a girl are lost in the woods, they eat part of an old lady's house and then they throw the old lady into an oven where she burns to death."

"No, I'm sorry, Grimm. We couldn't handle anything like that. But, I'll tell you what. I know this guy out in Hollywood. He might be able to get you a job writing for *S.W.A.T.*"

"I already tried them."

"Yeah?"

"They said my stuff was too gory."

Ms. Goose for the Seventies

Aug. 2, 1975

The trouble with children's literature, Jane Williamson feels, is that a great deal of it is irrelevant.

Ms. Williamson, who visited Wright State University earlier this week, is a managing editor for Feminist Press. As such, she is basically concerned with sexism in children's stories, advocating such alternatives as "A Train for Jane" and "William's Doll."

But the problem of relevancy also bothers her.

"If most children's books just portrayed reality," she insists, "that would be a big step. Think of how many children are affected by divorce, which is a subject that is almost entirely ignored in children's books."

Not all kiddy lit is out of step. There is, for instance, the updated jingle that goes:

"There was an old lady who lived in a shoe,

She had so many children, she didn't know what to do.

So she fed them all Spaghetti-Os and sent them to bed."

But that's an exception and it's gotta be tough for a lot of today's kids to identify with those old Mother Goose rhymes. Like, the kid who reads about Little Miss Muffett surely must wonder why he never sees tuffets advertised at Levitz. And how often do they get to order curds and whey at McDonald's?

And so, in the interest of relevance, let's bring Ms. Goose into the '70s.

For instance:

Mary, Mary, quite contrary
How does your garden grow?
With silver bells and cockleshells,
And tall green cannabis all in a row.

* * *

A dillar, a dollar
A ten o'clock scholar,
What makes you come so soon?
You used to come at ten o'clock,
But since they started busing,
You don't get here till noon.

* * *

Little Boy Blue come blow your horn,
The sheep's in the meadow, the cow's in the corn.
Where is the little boy tending the sheep?
He's off in Washington lobbying for higher price supports.

* * *

Tom, Tom, the piper's, son,
Stole a pig and away did run.
The pig was eat and Tom was beat,
And the ACLU did start to bleat.

* * *

To market, to market, to buy a fat pig,
Home again, home again, without any swine.
To market, to market to buy a fat hog,
A pound of pork is a buck twenty nine.

* * *

Rub-a-dub-dub, three men in a tub,
And who do you think they be?
The butcher, the baker
And a CIA agent posing as a candlestick maker.

* * *

Polly put the kettle on,
Polly put the kettle on,

Polly put the kettle on,
We'll all have some tea.
Sukey take it off again,
Sukey take it off again,
Sukey take it off again,
The cops are on their way.

* * *

Old Mother Hubbard went to the cupboard,
To fetch her poor dog a bone;
But when she got there, the cupboard was bare,
Because older persons on fixed incomes are always hit the
hardest.

* * *

Georgie Porgie, pudding and pie,
Kissed the girls and made them cry;
His lawyer said t'was an aberration,
The judge agreed and gave him shock probation.

Oh, Yummy! Poached Roach

May 22, 1975

NEWS ITEM: A University of Wisconsin professor says that insects may be the answer to any future world food crisis. He says they have more protein than meat, fewer calories than vegetables and are cheaper than either.

★ ★ ★

The year is 2012. John Doe (not his real name) pulls his car into the garage of his $400,000 lower middle class home after a hard day at work. He walks into the kitchen, kisses his wife and peeks through the glass window of the antiquated microwave oven.

"Oh no," he grumbles, "not roast mosquito again. Darn it, Jane, that's four times this week we've had mosquito. Fried mosquito, broiled mosquito, mosquito pot pie, mosquitos and beans. I'm getting sick of it."

"Well," his wife says defensively, "if you'd make more money in that crummy job of yours we'd be able to eat better. What do you expect on $3,000 a week, ladybugs?"

"All right, all right, don't start that again. I told you the boss says I'll get a raise as soon as this temporary recession is over. Course, what does he care? He's probably sitting down right now to a big, thick dragonfly steak."

The Does adjourn to the living room. Mr. Doe plops down in his chair and picks up the newspaper. He scans the front page.

The day's top story is about the impending marriage of Jacqueline Kennedy Onassis Sinatra to the world's richest man, J. Paul Orkin.

In Kansas, flea farmers are threatening to withhold their livestock from the market until prices go up. "People just don't realize how expenses have soared," one flea farmer is quoted as saying. "Why, do you know how much it costs to feed them now? The price of dogs is out of sight."

In Minnesota, Sen. Hubert Humphrey has announced plans to run for the presidency again. His campaign slogan will be "A cockroach in every pot."

Mr. Doe's reading is interrupted by Mrs. Doe, who wants to know if he'd like to go on a picnic this weekend.

"We could stop at the Colonel's and pick up a bucket of Southern fried boll weevils," she says hopefully.

"Oh, I don't know, dear," Mr. Doe replies. "The last time we went on a picnic it was such a disaster, remember? We tried half a dozen spots and still couldn't find any ants.

"Anyway, I was sort of thinking of going hunting this weekend. Locust season opens Saturday. Which reminds me, have you seen my fly swatter?"

"No dear. But I really wish you wouldn't go hunting. It's so dangerous. Just last week I read about a man who was swatted 12 times by hunters who mistook him for a hornet."

"Oh, don't worry about it. I've been going hunting since '96 and I haven't been swatted yet. '96, remember that year?"

"Of course I remember '96. That's the year we got married. We were so poor."

"Yeah, we sure were. But I wish we hadn't had to eat my butterfly collection."

"Oh I almost forgot," Mrs. Doe says suddenly. "I have terrific news. I was down in the basement today and guess what?"

"What?"

"We have termites."

"You're not kidding, are you?"

"No, it's true. Isn't that wonderful?"

"Boy, that's the first good news I've had this week."

Mr. Doe's elation is cut short by the sound of his wife yelling to their son in the family room.

"Junior Doe, you close that door. Do you want to let all the bugs out? And you better not be eating any flies. I warned you before about snacks before din . . . ohmygosh, dinner. I forgot all about it."

She runs to the kitchen and flings open the oven door. Thick smoke billows out.

"Oh no," she wails, "dinner is ruined."

"Don't worry about it, dear," Mr. Doe says consolingly. "I'll just go out and scrape something off the windshield."

There's a Worm in My Cookie

Oct. 23, 1975

Edith: *I was going to make your father a tongue sandwich, but he said he wouldn't eat nothing that came out of a cow's mouth.*

Gloria: *What are you making for him instead?*

Edith: *Eggs.*

★ ★ ★

Archie Bunker isn't the only one with funny ideas about food. Out in California, if the wire service report is to be believed, people are eating worms.

"They make excellent eating for people," declares Ronald Gaddie, president of North American Bait Farms Inc. of Ontario, Calif. Among the delicacies recommended by his company are redworm cookies.

But what if this idea worms its way into American menus? We'll have *Family Circle* running features about worms ("101 ways to add taste appeal to those leftover wrigglers" and "Betty Ford tells why they don't have tapeworms on the White House menu anymore"). A whole new field will be unearthed for Col. Sanders ("Get mom out of the kitchen, bring home a bucket of worms"). Restaurants will offer Surf 'N Turf Specials (one sludge worm, one night crawler, potato, salad and coffee).

And, of course, there will be worm cooking contests.

"Hi again, everybody, and welcome to the first Wonderful World of Worms Cook-Off. I'm here with our WRGL microphone to bring you all the action and highlights, every inch, every angle. A wide variety of dishes have been entered, so while we're waiting for the judges to announce the winners, let's walk around and talk with some of the contestants.

"Pardon me, sir, that looks like an interesting dish. What do you call it?"

"Grub steak."

"I see. Well, I've had steaks in some pretty grubby restaurants (heh, heh), what makes yours different?"

"Real grubs."

"Uh, very interesting. Well, let's move right along. Here's a lady with some unusual looking pastries. Would you tell us what these are, ma'am?"

"These are redworm turnovers."

"Redworm turnovers, eh? And could I ask you to share the secret of preparing them with our radio audience?"

"They're very simple, really. You just make your basic turnover dough and fill them with about a half dozen redworms each."

"And that's all there is to it?"

"Oh, land sakes, no. Then you have to stick them in the oven at 425 degrees and wait."

"Wait. Wait for what?"

"Wait for the worms to turn."

"Thank you. Well, I see we have another gentleman contestant. His specialty appears to be some sort of a spaghetti dish. Tell us, sir, what made you decide to enter this contest?"

"Contest? What contest? I'm on my way over to the lake to go fishing. And I'll thank you to keep your hands off my bait bucket."

"Oh, sorry about that."

"Ah, here's a lady with a savory-smelling worm casserole. This looks like a very complicated dish. You must have used all sorts of utensils in preparing it."

"Oh, goodness no. Just the ordinary, everyday kitchen things: grater, blender, double boiler, shovel."

"I see, and . . . what's that? Oh. If you'll excuse me, ma'am, I understand the judges are about to announce the winner of the first Wonderful World of Worms Cook-Off. Wait a minute, wait a minute, there seems to be some sort of commotion over at the judges' stand. Let's see if we can get a microphone over there and find out what's happening.

"Sir, sir, can you tell our audience what the problem is?"

"Oh, it's terrible. Just terrible."

"What's terrible, sir?"

"Well, you see, we were just about to announce the winner. It was Mrs. Earl E. Bird of Maggot, N.D., who made some simply marvelous earthworm cookies. And just as we were ready to announce her name, it happened."

"What happened?"

"Her cookies . . . they slithered away."

Count Hamstring's Revenge

Oct. 9, 1976

No one is really sure how ballet started.

Most experts agree, however, it was invented in the year 1237 by Count Philippe Bertrand Gaston de la Hamstring, known throughout the kingdom as Philippe the Clumsy.

Philippe was an awkward lad, which caused him to spend a rather unhappy childhood. His only achievement as a teen-ager was being named the most improved player on his high school jousting team. Four years in a row. As a senior, he was voted most likely to fatally injure himself while cleaning his bow and arrow.

In adulthood, however, Philippe became rich and successful as a manufacturer of chastity belts.

The secret of his success was that Philippe sold his chastity belts for just three francs each. The belts, you see, were merely loss leaders. The real money was in the keys, which Philippe sold for 28,000 gold Louies.

For every chastity belt he sold to the lord of the manor, Philippe could count on selling at least six keys. Maybe more if the lord of the manor was off fighting in a crusade somewhere.

Despite his success, Philippe was a bitter man, tormented by the knowledge that people still laughed at him behind his back because of his clumsiness. So for 36 years he schemed and plotted ways to strike back at them.

Finally, on a cold October day in 1237, a proclamation was nailed to the tavern door in the village square.

One million gold Louies, it said, would be awarded to any person in the kingdom who could exactly duplicate the set of physical positions shown at the bottom of the proclamation.

The people looked at the drawings of the positions at the bottom of the proclamation and saw that they were strange and unnatural. But they eagerly set about to try and duplicate them, because with one million gold Louies you could buy just about every chastity belt key in the kingdom.

And soon the land was filled with the sounds of tearing muscles and popping cartilage and shouts of, "Marie, hurry up with that liniment, will ya?"

Up in his castle, meanwhile, Count Philippe Bertrand Gaston de la Hamstring watched it all and laughed with glee as the people who had called him clumsy behind his back tried to twist and turn their bodies into positions that bodies were not meant to be twisted and turned into.

It was the highlight of Philippe's life. Unfortunately, he was not able to savor it for long. Because that very night, while cleaning his bow and arrow, he accidentally shot himself in the back.

Thus the world lost a super chastity belt salesman. But it gained a new word: Ballet. which, of course, means "Hamstring's revenge."

The reason I know all this is that just the other day I made my debut with the Dayton Ballet Company at Courthouse Square.

I was there at the request of the Friends of the Dayton Ballet Co., which was promoting its upcoming season and felt that having a bunch of celebrities doing ballet things would be a good way to get free publicity.

Unfortunately, the celebrities all chickened out, so Channel 7's Gil Whitney and I showed up instead.

"We'll just have you and Gil do a few basic positions at the barre with the dancers," is how it was explained to me.

(Barre, incidentally, is a French word. It means "place where you stand while you tear every ligament in your body.")

When the dancers arrive, we take our places at the barre. In front of me is a young man named Ron Hollenkamp, who is so agile that he can get in and out of an MG Midget without swearing. Behind me is a young lady named Judy Denman, who can scratch the back of her head with her foot.

"Let's start with a plie," touring company director Jon Rodriguez says.

(Plie is a French word. It means, "put your heels together, squat down, smile and pretend that you enjoy searing pains in your thighs.")

After that, we do the battement.

(Battement is a French word. It means, "bring your leg up over your head, hold it there for about an hour and hope that the seams in your trousers are sturdy.")

We top it off with a porte de bras.

(Porte de bras are three French words. They mean, "put your hands on your hips, bend forward at the waist, touch your forehead to your knees and remain in that position until the chiropractor arrives.")

It is while I am straining to reach this position (putting my hands on my hips has always been a tough one) that I hear it. It is faint, but it is unmistakable.

It is the ghost of Count Philippe Bertrand Gaston de la Hamstring. He is laughing his head off.

Sorry, But a Fat Old Guy Isn't Quite Right

Dec. 14, 1976

Dr. Clement Clarke Moore
Chelsea Farm
New York, N.Y.

Dear Dr. Moore:
Thank you for submitting your promotional suggestion to Creative Retailing and Sales Services Inc.

All of us here at CRASS were intrigued with the idea of a

fictional character that could be used to promote Christmas sales.

At a meeting of our advisory board, however, several issues were raised concerning your concept.

Dr. Snavely, of our medical department, wondered, for instance, why you conceptualize the character as a fat, elderly male.

He pointed out that in 37.8 percent of all fatal heart attacks among bearded Caucasian males over the age of 50, excess weight played an important role.

Not only is your character clearly overweight, Dr. Snavely noted, but he also smokes a pipe, increasing his risk on the actuarial tables.

Ms. Sternly, our vice president in charge of equality, objected to the fact that your character is a male, pointing out that our holidays are already rife with sexist stereotypes, including the Jack O'Lantern and Tom Turkey.

This, of course, prompted a lively rejoinder from our Mr. Johnson, who objected to the fact that your character is white, pointing out that we already have a white Easter bunny.

Following a thorough discussion of this matter, it was agreed that a possible solution to the problem would be to slightly alter your character.

Instead of a single white male, it could be revised into a racially and sexually homogeneous squad to consist of: one (1) white male, one (1) white female, one (1) black male, one (1) black female and one (1) Chicano of indeterminate sex.

This proposal was set aside for further consideration, pending decisions on several other points.

The most pressing of these additional questions concerned your character's Christmas Eve activities which, if I read your outline correctly, consist of surreptitiously entering inhabited dwellings at night.

Quite frankly, Dr. Moore, I blue-pencilled this idea without even bothering to show it to the board.

Instead of having your character sliding down the chimney, I recommend that he be depicted knocking at the front door, showing proper identification and waiting on the doorstep, if necessary, while his credentials are checked with the Better Business Bureau and the local police department.

Even with this change, however, certain legal questions remain.

Is the merchandise your character distributes approved by the Consumer Products Safety Commission? If not, will he accept liability in the event of injury due to faulty workmanship?

Not only do you fail to address these important questions, Dr. Moore, but you also seem to give implicit approval to reckless driving, illegal parking and disturbing the peace in the manner with which your character arrives and departs.

Which brings up the additional question of your character's vehicle.

Is it an automobile? If so, is it equipped with seat belts? An exhaust emission control? An interlock system?

Or is it an airplane, in which case it would have to be established that your character had received sufficient dual instruction hours to qualify for his solo permit and that he had filed a proper flight plan.

Also, we are advised by the SPCA that they do not look favorably upon the idea of reindeer working the entire night without a break. They insist on fresh reindeer every hour, or every 100,000 rooftops, whichever comes first.

In view of these difficulties and unresolved questions, Dr. Moore, it is the decision of our advisory board that the character you envision is not a viable concept.

Sincerely,
G. Fernwood Chumley
Marketing Director
Creative Retailing and Sales Services Inc.

Yule Be Sorry You Read This

Dec. 25, 1976

A Christmas story:

It was a mild December night in Moscow.

Rudolph Sergei Illyovich and his wife, Olga, were taking their after-dinner walk through Red Square. Rudolph and Olga always took a walk after dinner. They had taken their first after-dinner walk as newlyweds nearly 20 years ago, on the day Olga prepared their first meal. Taking a walk afterwards was Rudolph's idea. He said it helped relieve the pain.

At 42, Rudolph Sergei Illyovich had become successful enough to be comfortable, but not enough to come under suspicion.

He was a member in good standing of the Communist Party and was employed at the Mustrop Borscht Co. Five years ago, during the company's annual slogan contest, he had submitted: "If we make a better Mustrop, the world will beet a path to our door."

As a result of the suggestion, Rudolph Sergei Illyovich was named assistant inspector at Plant B. He had been inspector-in-chief.

Olga Illyovich grew up on a farm outside Rybinsk. She was always a husky lass and as a teenager she pulled the plow on the horse's day off. One day, as she was working the front 40, the Peoples' District Commissioner happened by. He was upset when he saw Olga pulling a plow.

"Pulling a plow is not fit work for a young girl," the Peoples' District Commissioner told Olga's parents. So he took her to Moscow to pull streetcars.

It was on the Gorkei St. run that Rudolph Sergei Illyovich first saw Olga. He was riding. She was pulling. Sweat coursed down her face. Dark stains circled under the arms of her uniform. Finally, Rudolph Sergei Illyovich could stand it no more. He got off the streetcar and walked up to Olga.

"Comrade," he said, "a little anti-perspirant wouldn't hurt."

Six months later they were married.

Their 20 years together proved to be happy ones, marred only by their inability to have children. Rudolph Sergei Illyovich blamed Olga for that. She was the one who insisted that he carry her across the threshold on their wedding night.

Now, as they walked, precipitation began to fall.

"Look, dear," Olga said, "it is beginning to snow. I love it when it snows during our after-dinner walks, don't you?"

"Yes, my own sweet Clydesdale," Rudolph Sergei Illyovich replied. "But that is not snow. It is rain."

"Oh, no," Olga insisted, "it is snow."

"I do not want to argue with you," said Rudolph Sergei Illyovich, who really did not want to argue with her, seeing as how she outweighed him by 257 pounds. "But it is definitely rain."

That disagreement continued until eventually they found themselves in front of a Peoples' Phone Booth.

"I have an idea," said Rudolph Sergei Illyovich, "why don't we call the Peoples' Television Station and ask the weatherman. He can settle this for us."

Olga agreed. It was decided that Rudolph Sergei Illyovich would place the call. The last time Olga entered a Peoples' Phone Booth, she had to be helped out by the Peoples' Rescue Squad.

"Hello," said Rudolph Sergei Illyovich when he got through to the Peoples' Television Station. "I would like to speak please with the Peoples' Weatherman."

His call was transferred.

"Yes," snapped Nikoli Breckovichski, Moscow's only licensed meteorologist, when the phone rang. Nikoli Breckovichski was not in a good mood. He had blown the weather forecast five of the last six days. One more blunder and he would be transferred to the UHF station in Murmansk.

Nikoli Breckovichski wished that he could be an imperialist capitalist and live in the United States. In the United States, he had heard, weathermen who blew the forecasts wound up with their own late night shows in the summer.

"I am sorry to disturb you, Comrade," Rudolph Sergei Illyovich said. "But I would like to know, if you please, is it at this moment snowing, or is it raining?"

Nikoli Breckovichski grumbled at being bothered by such a call, but he hid his irritation. It would not do to alienate a viewer. The Peoples' Television Station was getting clobbered in the ratings as it was. Nikoli Breckovichski shuddered to think of what would happen if there was another station in town.

"One moment, Comrade," he said to Rudolph Sergei Illyovich, "I will check the Peoples' Meteorological Instruments."

Nikoli Breckovichski walked across the room and stuck his

hand out the window. A moment later he was back on the phone.

"It is now raining, Comrade," Nikoli Breckovichski told Rudolph Sergei Illyovich.

"Would you repeat that for my wife, please?" Rudolph Sergei Illyovich asked, holding the receiver out of the Peoples' Phone Booth so that Olga could hear.

"It is now raining," Nikoli Breckovichski repeated.

"Thank you, Comrade," Rudolph Sergei Illyovich said, hanging up the Peoples' Phone.

Rudolph Sergei Illyovich and his wife continued their walk in silence. It was not until they arrived at the door of their Peoples' Condominiums that Olga finally spoke.

"I am sorry to have doubted you, Rudolph Sergei Illyovich," she said. "But I could have sworn that it was snow."

"It was a natural mistake, my little Percheron," said Rudolph Sergei Illyovich. "But I am surprised that you would question my word on this matter. After all, surely you must know by now that Rudolph the Red knows rain, dear."

Porky Pig for the Defense of Larry

Jan. 15, 1977

NEWS ITEM: Mel Blanc, the voice of Bugs Bunny, Porky Pig, Daffy Duck and dozens of other cartoon characters, is listed as a possible defense witness in the obscenity trial of *Hustler* magazine publisher Larry Flynt . . .

★ ★ ★

"If it please the court, defense would like to call its next witness."

"Proceed."

"The defense calls Porky Pig."

"The bailiff will swear the witness."

"Raise your right hand. Do you swear to tell the truth, the whole truth and nothing but the truth?"

"I duh-I duh-I duh . . . sure."

"Please state your full name and occupation."

"Porky Pig, mov-mov-mov . . . actor."

"Be seated."

"Mr. Pig, are you now or have you ever appeared in an obscene movie?"

"No."

"May I remind you, Mr. Pig, that you are under oath?"

"But I nev-I nev-I nev . . . I didn't do it."

"At this time, your honor, defense would like to introduce into evidence Exhibit A, a movie entitled *Porky Brings Home the Bacon.* Do you remember that movie, Mr. Pig?"

"I cer-I cert-I cert . . . you bet."

"And you remember what you wore in that movie?"

"Well, I wore the same thing I always wear. My blue jacket and my red tie."

"What else?"

"Nothing else."

"You mean to say, Mr. Pig, that you appeared in the movie with no pants on?"

"But, I never wear pa-pa-pa . . . trousers."

"You mean to sit there, without your pants, I might add, and tell this court that you do not consider it obscene to appear in public and on film with no pants on?"

"Bu-bu-bu . . ."

"Let me ask you something else, Mr. Pig. Do you remember the name of your co-star in that movie?"'

"Yes."

"What was her name?"

"Petunia Pig."

"Is it the same Petunia pig who starred in the recent X-rated films *Behind the Green Boar* and *Deep Shoat?*"

"Objection. That question is incompetent, irrelevant and immaterial."

"Sustained."

"Sorry, your honor. Tell me, Mr. Pig, what did Ms. Pig wear in that movie, the one in which you pranced around in front of the camera with your bare . . ."

"Objection."

"Sustained."

"What did Ms. Pig wear?"

"I can't rem-I can't rem-I can't rem . . . I forget."

"Perhaps I can refresh your memory, Mr. Pig. Were her hocks covered?"

"No."

"Her loins?"

"No."

"Her chops?"

"No."

"Objection, your honor. Defense counsel is badgering the witness."

"Overruled. However, attorney for the defense has made his point. The court suggests that he move along to another line of questioning."

"Certainly, your honor. Tell me, Mr. Pig, who else appeared in this movie?"

"Well, there was Yosemite Sam, Bugs Bunny, Daffy Duck . . ."

"Mr. Bunny and Mr. Duck, did they wear any clothing?"

"No, but . . ."

"In other words, Mr. Pig, this movie, which you claim was not obscene, included yourself appearing without pants, a female displaying partial frontal nudity and two other males of a questionable relationship who appeared throughout the movie totally naked."

"Yes, but, it's not the way you make it sound. That movie wasn't porna-porna-porna . . . dirty."

"I have no more questions, Mr. Pig. You may step down.

"For my next witness, your honor, I call Elmer Fudd."

"Elmer Fudd to the stand. Do you swear to tell the truth, the whole truth and nothing but the truth?"

"I pwomise I will tell the whole twuth . . ."

A Labor Day Fable

Sept. 4, 1976

Once upon a time there was a man who lived in a far-away land.

Men in fables, you will notice, always live in far-away lands, never in the land next door. No one knows why this is.

In any event, this man spent a great deal of his time wondering about things. He wondered why the grass was green. He wondered why the sky was blue. He wondered why columnists are so miserably underpaid.

But mostly he wondered about people. Where, he wondered, do the strangest people in all the world live.

Finally he could stand the wondering no more. And so he left his home, vowing that he would not return until he had found the strangest people in all the world.

It is not known what his wife thought when she woke up and learned that he had gone. But it is possible that she did not mind all that much, because men who sit around wondering all day tend to make lousy husbands, anyway.

The man's journey took him to many strange lands.

It took him to a land where it was said that all the people worked together, each one sharing in the fruits of their common labor. But soon the man noticed that a few people always seemed to get more fruit than others.

And his jouney took him to a land where the people worshiped a god of love and peace . . . and blew up people who didn't worship the same.

In due time the man's journey brought him to a land of vast wealth, a land richer than all the other lands he had visited before.

Everywhere he looked in this prosperous land the man saw people with great amounts of money. And so he observed the people of this land closely, to see how they spent their wealth.

Many of the people, he discovered, spent their money to watch other people play games. There were games in which men put on suits of plastic armor and bumped into each other a lot. There were games in which a man threw a ball at another man who was holding a stick. There were games in which tall men in their underwear threw a ball through an iron hoop.

The man didn't understand these games, but he knew that they must be very important, because the people of the land paid vast amounts of money to watch them.

But not all of the people paid money to see these games, the man learned. Some of the people turned up their noses at the games. Many of these people spent their money on things like musical shows put on by men and women in funny clothes.

At first it troubled the man that he could not understand the words that the men and women in the funny clothes were singing. But then he realized that the people who paid to see the shows didn't understand them, either, and it didn't seem to bother them. After every performance they jumped to their feet anyway, clapping their hands and yelling, "Bravo." Even the ones who had slept through the whole thing.

The man who wondered found all of these things a little odd, but not really strange.

Then one day, just about the time he had decided to move on in his search for the strangest people in all the world, the man saw something that really made him wonder.

It was a television show, in which a man in fancy clothes was asking people to send him money. The man in the fancy clothes smoked a lot and appeared to be very tired, as if he had not slept all night.

"Why is that man in the fancy clothes doing that?" the man who wondered asked one of the people who lived in the land of vast wealth.

"Oh, he's conducting a telethon," he was told.

"A telethon? What is a telethon?"

"A telethon is when some guys go on television and try to talk people into sending them money."

"I see. And what do they do with this money?"

"Well, they spend it on diseases and stuff like that. You know, the ones that kill kids, or maybe make 'em crippled."

At first, the man who wondered was certain that he had misunderstood.

"It is obvious that we are having what will some day be known as a communication gap," he said. "Because it sounded as if you said that the people in this wealthy land must be begged for money to keep their own children from being killed and crippled."

"Yeah, well, you got it about right, Mac. Don't ask me to explain it. Anyway, I'm too busy to worry about it right now. I gotta get down and buy tickets so I can watch 'em hit some balls with sticks."

And the man who wondered walked away, shaking his head. He still could not believe what he had just heard.

But there was one good thing about it, he decided, finally.

At least his search was over.

The Trouble with Horror Films

May 13, 1976

They showed *The Birds* on TV again the other night, which, as you doubtless know, is the tender and poignant story of how a bunch of sea gulls tried to eat California. (Not to be confused with *Jaws*, the tender and poignant story of how a shark tried to eat New England).

In any event, it is a fairly decent flick. But, like most other scary flicks, not very scary.

The problem with scary movies is that they hardly ever deal with real people in real settings. I mean, when's the last time you saw an eight-foot guy with a bolt in his neck walking down Ludlow Street? When's the last time you saw a werewolf in a tuxedo running around Kettering Field? When's the last time you saw an invisible man?

And even the ones that do have real-type people mess it up, because they're always taking place in settings that most people have never seen, like run-down Southern mansions owned by Bette Davis.

Now it seems to me that if they wanted to make a really scary movie, they'd fill it with real people. It seems to me they'd put it in a setting that people could identify with.

It seems to me they'd make a movie like:

Whatever happened to Martha Schwartz?

The setting is a Gothic, three-bedroom split-level in Beavercreek. It is twilight and eerie music from an unseen television set fills the air.

A pale, haggard man sits in a Strato-lounger, where he has been confined for the last 37 years. A woman shuffles toward him. She is a terrifying sight. She wears a shapeless bathrobe, floppy slippers and curlers in her hair. She is carrying a covered tray.

Malice glitters in her eyes as she thrusts the tray forward

at the cringing soul in the chair. Slowly, fearfully, he lifts the cover.

The man screams and recoils in horror at what he sees. "Aaarrghhh."

The woman throws back her head, a wild cackle erupting from her throat. "Ah-heh-heh-heh."

The eerie music builds to a crescendo. ("Hold the pickle, hold the lettuce . . .")

The camera zooms in on the tray that has fallen from the man's trembling hands. Closer, closer, until it reveals . . . macaroni and cheese.

Whimpering now, the man speaks.

"P-p-please, Martha, not again. I'm begging you in the name of mercy, not again. I just can't take anymore."

He breaks down into wild, uncontrollable sobbing, but the woman is unmoved.

"You can't stand it!" she shrieks. "You can't stand it! How do you think I've felt all these years? You stole my youth and my beauty from me, forcing me to stay here in this horrible place, never making enough money at the crummy job of yours so that I could afford to buy decent food. I told you to get a real job. But, no, you had to be a newspaper columnist.

"Well, this is what you get for it, you sniveling wretch. It serves you right."

Cackling grotesquely, the woman shuffles out of the room, leaving the sniveling wretch in his chair, where he snivels wretchedly.

The eerie music builds to another crescendo. ("Kool-Aid, Kool-Aid, tastes great, Kool-Aid, Kool-Aid, can't wait.")

Then it is night. The camera focuses on the man. He is out of his chair now, crawling up the stairs slowly, painfully, his legs rendered useless from 37 years of sitting in his Strato-lounger watching *Bowling for Dollars.*

Finally he reaches the top of the stairs. He crawls to the bedroom where, sleeping on her back, snoring loudly, Martha lies.

The camera zooms in on the man's left hand to show that he is clutching a five-pound box of Delmonico elbow macaroni.

Quivering with excitement, he opens the box and takes out one macaroni.

While eerie music drifts up from downstairs ("You can trust your car to the man who wears the star . . .") he drops the hard, dry macaroni into the woman's gaping mouth. With a small choking sound, it slips down her throat.

The man drops in another piece of macaroni. And another. And another. Eventually the entire five-pound box of hard, dry macaroni is empty.

Then the man reaches into his pocket and pulls out a hot banana pepper. Trembling with excitement, he watches it slither past her tongue.

Satisfied then, he falls back on the bed and waits.

Finally the woman awakens. Her hand goes to her throat. Her expression indicates that she is terribly thirsty. Groggily, she gets out of the bed and stumbles to the bathroom.

The sound of running water can be heard, followed by gulping. More running water, more gulping. Running water, gulping. But the camera remains focused on the face of the man. He is smiling evilly as he pictures the effect of all that water when it hits five pounds of hard, dry macaroni.

Suddenly, there is an enormous explosion in the bathroom.

In the bed, there is a wild, demented laugh. "Ah-hah-hah-hah."

The picture fades. The eerie music builds to its final crescendo.

("Plop, plop, fizz, fizz, oh what a relief it is . . .")

He Comes by It Honestly, Folks

Jan. 27, 1977

Under the influence of the current televising of *Roots,* I set about the other day to reconstruct a little of my own family's history in an effort to find out how I got this way and who to blame.

All I was able to find out about my old man was that he grew up in Oil City, Pa., where each morning he got up, stoked the furnace, shoveled the snow and walked two miles in bitter cold to get to school.

Information was easier to uncover on my mother's side, mostly because my mother's side of the family always talked a lot more.

My mother's maiden name was Eridon. She grew up in Cleveland, where each morning she got up, chopped a cord of wood, shoveled an acre of snow and walked through a blizzard to get to school.

My mother's father, for whom I invented the pet name "Grandpa," was an immigrant. He grew up in Rumania, where each morning he got up, chopped down a forest in Bacau, shoveled off the Carpathian Mountains and walked through World War I to get to school.

His name was George Eridon and he died when I was young, leaving me with only a few scattered memories. He was, I recall, a baker by trade, and he helped make rye bread at the Laub Bakery. He was rather short, with a round face, a small mustache and the tip of one finger missing.

The finger was a source of constant mystery to me, until one day I finally worked up the courage to ask him about it.

"Grandpa, how did you hurt your finger?"

"It was an accident at the bakery. It was cut off by the slicer."

"What happened to the part that was cut off?"

"It was never found."

Since that day, I have not cared much for rye bread.

Grandpa Eridon had a brother, who was known to everyone as "Uncle." Uncle's wife was called "Auntie." That seemed to be the most reasonable arrangement.

Uncle was a big man, but quiet. That was because Auntie was a small woman, but mouthy. The only time Auntie was not mouthy was when she was riding in a car. Riding in a car frightened Auntie so much that she was unable to talk.

When he died, Uncle's car had 136,000 miles on it.

My mother's mother's maiden name was Schaefer and she grew up in Valley City, Ohio, where every morning she got up, saw how cold it was and went back to bed. That is why she is still going strong at the age of 77.

The Schaefer line extends back into Germany and tracing it proved to be difficult, what with the Hapsburgs always mad at the Hohenzollern's and the Junkers acting all snooty and all of them running over to invade France every couple of weeks and forgetting to keep the records.

With the help of the Schaefer family Bible, I was able to trace back four generations, to an account of the death of my great-great-great-grandmother Erma Schaefer in 1856.

The story, written by Hans Schaefer, the younger of her two sons, is rambling. In places, it is illegible. But I found it well worth the effort of having it translated and I hope you, too, will find it interesting.

Here is Hans Schaefer's account:

"17 August 1856.

"Our beloved Mama, Erma Clara Schaefer, nee Weissbrodt, passed on to her reward this day. The (illegible) of her passing are painful to recount, but I must persist.

"After mass this morning my elder brother, Alois, and myself helped Mama into the wagon and, as always, took her for the Sabbath morning ride into the lovely (illegible) mountains that border our village to the north.

"It was one of the few pleasures left to Mama, being plagued by the infirmities of advancing age and frequently possessed of the ague. But these rides seemed ever to renew her spirits and return the bright flush of youth to her wrinkled cheeks. It was ever joy to hear her pleased (illegible) as we rode ever higher into the mountains and she was able to peer over the side of the wagon into the valley far below.

"But our path was narrow and the mountains steep, preventing me from witnessing her happiness. It took my every (illegible) just to keep the wagon on the road.

"Thus, I never knew when the hand of Providence stepped in. I was unaware that our beloved Mama had leaned too far over the side of the wagon and had fallen (illegible). Nor did I learn of it until my brother, Alois, perchanced to glance into the back of the wagon and shouted, with great agitation:

"Look, Hans, no Ma."

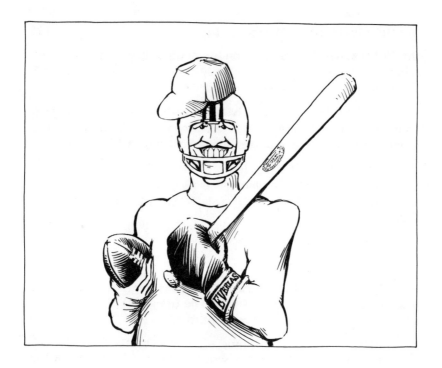

5 The Games That Grown Men Play

I always liked sports, even before Howard Cosell invented them.

I began my newspaper career as a sports writer, going to Super Bowls and World Series and Masters golf tournaments, discovering that the people who played in them were wise men and fools, princes and knaves.

After 10 years I wanted a change, so I left the sports department and moved to the "real world," which I found to be populated with wise men and fools, princes and knaves.

Who's Crazy, Me or Those Sox Fans?

Oct. 16, 1975

CINCINNATI — It is a strange and wondrous place, this world of sports.

What else can be said about a world in which a man spends $350 for something that is free and when you ask him why, he responds:

"Are you crazy?"

Mike LaFoley is the name of the most recent gentleman to raise that question. He is 27 years old, married and the owner of a hardware store in Acton, Mass.

He is not rich, he says. But he has laid out $202 for an airplane ticket, $21 a night for a motel room, who knows how much for meals and refreshments and $45 for tickets to baseball games that are being shown for free on televison.

And he has he nerve to ask me if I'm crazy.

Of course, these are not just any baseball games. These are World Series games, and to Mike LaFoley being at a World Series game is "the thrill of a lifetime."

So Mike LaFoley sits with two friends in Section 238 at Riverfront Stadium and risks the wrath of the local populace by cheering for the Boston Red Sox and considers himself fortunate to have been given the opportunity to spend $350 for something that is free.

But Mike LaFoley and his friends are not alone.

In section 438, Joe Cappeli stands up, cups his hands and yells in the direction of Boston batter Carlton Fisk: "C'mon, Pudge, baseball's just a game to these farmers."

Joe Cappeli, 29, is a fire fighter from Newton, Mass. Like Mike LaFoley, he has flown to Cincinnati with two of his friends. Flying coach, they paid $146 each for their plane fare. Their two motel rooms cost them $112. The Grand Prix they rented ran $64, plus mileage. They have each paid $50 for the tickets to the games that are being shown on television for free.

Even if the Dodgers had won the National League pennant and these games were being played in Los Angeles, Joe Cappeli says he would have made the trip.

"The Sox don't win too many pennants," he says in a voice

that is hoarse from yelling insults at the Cincinnati agrarians. "You never know when you're going to get another chance."

The same line of thought prompted a 26-year-old post office employe from Providence, R.I, to make the all-night drive to Cincinnati with his wife.

"You never know when they'll do it again," says the post office employe, whose name is John and who wears a painter's cap with the nicknames of the Boston players written on it.

John figures the trip will cost him about $400. He considers that a bargain.

"I was figuring about $30 each for tickets. That's what standing room is going for in Boston. Scalpers are getting $50 for seats up there and I've heard of some going as high as $100."

When he arrved in Cincinnati, John was able to buy two seats for $30. So already he's $30 ahead.

Despite a reported avalanche of requests, out-of-towners say tickets in Cincinnati are remarkably easy to come by.

"We got here 10 minutes before the game and bought $6 standing room tickets for $5," says Will, who skipped out on his job as a waiter in Boston and drove for 20 hours to get to Cincinnati. "I don't think the people here care much about the Series."

"I was willing to pay $25 for a ticket," says Tom, a college student whose home is in Foxboro, Mass., "but I got a standing room ticket for $6."

Not all of those who wear their $2.50 Boston caps and wave their $1.50 Boston pennants are from New England.

Dave, for instance, is from Athens, Ohio, but he is wearing a Red Sox cap.

"I'm not really a Boston fan," he says. "I'm a Mets fan. But Pittsburgh lost, so I gotta root for Boston."

Dave, it should be noted, is a beer distributor. Apparently he believes in his product. There is no other way to explain what he just said.

And there is Alex Browne, who is from Louisville, but who cheers for the Red Sox because many of the players on the Boston team once played minor league ball in his hometown. So he walks through the stands in Cincinnati wearing his Boston cap and his authentic Red Sox shirt that has not been washed since he got it in 1967.

And seeing him dressed like that, Pete Rose observes: "Keep your eye on that guy He's going to get his butt kicked before the night is over."

Alex Browne paid $10 for the privilege of walking around in Riverfront Stadium and running the risk of getting his butt kicked.

And Mike LaFoley wants to know if I'm crazy.

All the Answers on the World Series

Oct. 16, 1976

World Series questions and answers:

Q—What is the World Series?

A—The World Series is a series of baseball games staged by two semi-competing business firms. It consists of a minimum of four games, none of which is over until the last man is out.

Q—Why do they call it the World Series?

A—Because every country in the world is eligible to compete in it. Except for 157 of them.

Q—Are World Series games much different from regular season games?

A—Certainly. They are much more expensive.

Q—Why is the World Series sometimes referred to as the Fall Classic?

A—The term Fall Classic was invented in 1921 by a Chicago sports writer who was trying to convince his editors that the event was so important he just had to go to New York and cover it. After calling it the Fall Classic in 29 consecutive stories, the editors were convinced and the writer was dispatched to New York, where he was mugged outside the Polo Grounds.

Q—When was the first World Series game played?

A—The first World Series game was played in Philadelphia on the afternoon of Oct. 9, 1905. On Oct. 10, 1905, the first World Series office pool was put together.

Q—What business firms are competing in this year's World Series?

A—The Cincinnati Reds Inc. and the New York Yankees Inc.

Q—How did they qualify?

A—The Reds qualified by finishing with the best record in the National League's Western Division.

Q—Name another team in the Western Division?

A—Atlanta.

Q—After winning the Western Division, what did the Reds do?

A—They defeated the Philadelphia Phillies, who were the winners of the Eastern Division.

Q—Who are some of the teams in the Eastern Division?

A—Chicago and St. Louis.

Q—How did the New York Yankees qualify?

A—By winning the American League pennant.

Q—What is an American League? I have lived in this area all of my life and I never heard anything about an American League.

A—That's because it is only 75 years old.

Q—Is the National League better than the American League?

A—Absolutely.

Q—How do we know?

A—Because Pete Rose says so.

Q—Is there any other way of telling?

A—Of course. We know that the National League is vastly superior to the American League because it has won one of the last four World Series and 29 of 71 overall.

Q—Which business firm is favored this year?

A—Our Reds.

Q—Why do you call them our Reds?

A—Because they are playing their hearts out for the glory of the Cincinnati area.

Q—You mean, even if there was no money involved, they would be out there doing their best anyway?

A—Don't be ridiculous.

Q—Then why should I bother to cheer for the Reds?

A—Because anyone who cheers for the Reds stands for goodness, sportsmanship, fair play and truth. And Yankee fans, as we all know, are loudmouth, drunken vandals.

Q—What will we do when our Reds win the World Series?

A—We will all gather at Fountain Square, where we will yell, throw firecrackers at passing cars and get bombed out of our minds.

In the Press Box with an All-Pro Tackle

Oct. 30, 1973
(Reprinted in *Best Sports Stories,* E. P. Dutton, 1974)

"You know," the guy sitting next to me in the press box said, "it really baffles me. I can't understand what all these people are doing here."

The guy had a good point. It was a typical autumn day in Pittsburgh: cold, wet and ugly. The game was being shown on television. It really made no sense that 45,761 persons should sit in Three Rivers Stadium risking pneumonia to watch the Steelers play the Bengals.

Yep. The guy had a good point. What made the point sort of funny, though, was that the guy was Mike Reid.

Reid, the Bengals' all-pro defensive tackle, wasn't able to play against the Steelers. He thought on Friday that he could play. His injured back felt fine then. But Friday evening he was getting out of his car when something gave out in his back. The next thing he knew he was lying on the ground, unable to get up.

For almost half an hour he lay there, laughing at his predicament in spite of the pain. Laughing at the notions he had entertained just a few minutes earlier of playing a violent game of football.

Sunday Mike Reid was scratched from the Bengals lineup. He wanted to watch the game from the sidelines, but the team doctor wanted him to be someplace where it was warm. Someplace where there was a constant flow of hot air to loosen the muscles in his back. The press box was selected.

And so on Sunday I found myself sitting next to Mike Reid awaiting the showdown between the Bengals and Steelers.

What an opportunity. What better way to watch a football game than with an all-pro at your elbow? It was like going to a concert and sitting next to Van Cliburn.

I couldn't wait to hear Reid's expert commentary, his piercing insights. I was tired of sitting in the company of dullards who could only say things like "Boy, that fumble hurt."

Second down early in the game. Boobie Clark sweeps the right side, gains four yards and fumbles. The call is close. It seems like a slow whistle to me. I look at Reid, waiting expectantly for his opinion.

"Boy, that fumble hurt," he says.

Play progresses. Reid is silent. It's obvious he doesn't want to be a showoff and dazzle me with more technical talk than I could possibly hope to understand. But I decide to encourage him. Ken Anderson completes a 53-yard pass to Bob Trumpy.

"Say," I say. "Isn't that the same play you guys used for a touchdown against Detroit?"

"Don't ask me," Reid shrugs. "I don't know anything about the offense."

Deflated, but not discouraged, I keep my ears open for any meaningful comments as the game continues.

Essex Johnson juggles a pass, catches it, then fumbles at Cincinnati's 13. Another close call by the officials. It might have been an incomplete pass.

I look at Reid.

"Do you know where the word ukulele comes from?" he asks.

"No," I confess, trying to make the connection between ukulele and what just happened on the field.

"It comes from the Hawaiian word uku, which means flea, and lele, which means leaping."

"So?" I demand. "What's that got to do with Essex fumbling?"

"Nothing. That's just something I learned in my Funk and Wagnalls."

I thank him for his insight and resume watching the game.

Terry Bradshaw throws a pass that skips off the hands of Franco Harris. Tommy Casanova intercepts and runs five yards, then flips to Ken Riley. The Pittsburgh writers are screaming that it was a forward lateral.

"That's not right," Reid declares. "It couldn't have been a forward lateral, because there is no such thing. That's a contradiction in terms, if you stop and think about it."

Unable to cope with this logic, I turn to the dullard behind me and comment, "Boy, that interception hurt."

Later in the second quarter Bradshaw is injured trying to run the ball. As he comes off the field, Reid shouts out: "See there, Terry? God is punishing you for those things you wrote about me in your book." (Later, Reid asks for the quarterback's address so he can send him a get-well note.)

Then it's the final minute of the first half.

"The crowd is sure ubiquitous," Reid observes.

"Uquibitous?" a nearby writer repeats, obviously overwhelmed by the word. Reid chortles softly at the writer's ignorance. I join him in his laugh and make a mental note to look up ubiquitous when I get back to the office.

I also make a mental note not to sit next to Van Cliburn at any concerts.

The Inside Dope on the Super Bowl

Jan. 17, 1976

It's all very well and good to say, as the National Football League does over and over, that 75 million persons in this country will watch the Super Bowl on television tomorrow.

But what the league fails to point out is the inescapable fact that 137 million persons will not watch the Super Bowl on television tomorrow.

The reason for this appalling lack of interest, I believe, is that those 137 million persons don't really know enough about what's going on down there on the field. This is known to' psychologists as the Curt Gowdy Syndrome.

I mean, they've heard about the game and probably they've heard some of the technical jargon and esoteric statistics. But they haven't been exposed to the little insights that might make the game interesting to them.

And so, in an effort to make Super Bowl X a meaningful

event for those persons who could care less about crackback blocks and rotating zones, I am pleased to present this list of little known facts for first-time viewers.

The game

Super Bowl X matches the champion of the National Football Conference (NFC) against the champion of the American Football Conference (AFC). The winner will be recognized as the greatest football team in the United States of America (U.S.A.), except in Oklahoma and Columbus, Ohio.

The teams

The Pittsburgh Steelers, who allegedly were founded on race track winnings and now reign as champion of a league that is outspokenly opposed to gambling.

The Dallas Cowboys, whose general manager once was accused by an employe as being "sick, demented and totally dishonest." In reply, he said: "That's not bad, he got two out of three."

The coaches

Pittsburgh — Chuck Noll: Hobbies include gourmet cooking. Nicknamed "the Pope" during his playing days at the University of Dayton for reputed infallibility.

Dallas — Tom Landry: Hobbies include not smiling. Nicknamed "the plastic man" by a former employe for reputed fallibility. As a token of appreciation for the nickname, Mr. Landry thereupon fired the employe.

The quarterbacks

Pittsburgh — Terry Bradshaw: Has long blond hair flowing from under helmet. Has short pink skin inside of helmet. Hobbies include raising pigeons, which he describes as "a lot of fun, except for the crap." Met and married Miss Teen Age America in storybook romance. Storybook romance marred somewhat by subsequent divorce. Receives large volumes of fan mail. Noteworthy sample: "Dear Mr. Bradshaw: My husband and I watch you on t.v. and we think you are degenerate."

Dallas—Roger Staubach: Potential career as pianist ended at age 11 when he forgot William Tell Overture during recital.

During college career, once killed a groundhog with a thrown baseball at a distance of 90 feet. Suffered 17 separations of left shoulder before turning pro. Little finger on right hand permanently bent at 45-degree angle.

The running backs

Pittsburgh — Franco Harris: Only player in NFL ever kissed by Frank Sinatra, as far as anyone knows. Frenchy Fuqua: Claims to be French nobleman whose skin was turned dark brown by atomic blast while vacationing on the Riviera. Once attracted considerable attention for flashy wardrobe, which included platform shoes with live goldfish in the heels. No longer plays much, so nobody cares what he wears. Rocky Bleier: Caught shrapnel in leg during Vietnam shrapnel-catching contest.

Dallas—Robert Newhouse: Replaced veteran Walt Garrison, who once walked undetected through airport metal detecting device carrying 17 whittling knives.

The offensive linemen

Nobody cares about offensive linemen.

The defensive linemen

Pittsburgh—L.C. Greenwood: Wears shiny gold football shoes, but stands 6-foot-6 and weighs 245, so nobody ever says anything about it. "Mean" Joe Greene: Is not really mean. Dwight White: Is not really white.

Dallas—Bob Lilly: One of the all-time greats at his position, but not expected to have much impact on tomorrow's game inasmuch as he retired last year.

The linebackers

Nobody in his right mind makes fun of linebackers.

The defensive backs

Pittsburgh—Glen Edwards: Children's names are Landrick and Tanisia.

Dallas—Charlie Waters: Once broke his arm putting his shirt on. Cliff Harris: Attended Ouachita Baptist, which three out of four announcers can't pronounce.

The kickers

Pittsburgh—Roy Gerela: has smallest feet on Pittsburgh team. Bobby Walden: Had end of little toe amputated. Denies that he did it to make his feet smaller than Gerela's. Lives in Climax, Ga.

Dallas—Mitch Hoopes (pronounced Hups). Toni Fritsch (pronounced Fritsch). One of the best NFL players ever to come out of Vienna, Austria.

Paul Brown: I Only Thought I Knew Him

Jan. 6, 1976

Somehow I always figured that the next time Paul Brown quit coaching it would be accompanied by flowers and soft organ music and a long, slow ride in a black limousine.

After his being forced to hang up his cleats once, I just assumed they'd have to cut them off him this time.

Having spent seven seasons writing about the Cincinnati Bengals and their fabled creator, I thought I knew the man well and could predict his moves. I realize now that I don't know him at all. At least, I don't know him any better now than I did seven years ago.

Paul Brown is a hard man, I have been told, grim and forbidding. So I am nervous and just a little frightened when I walk into his office to interview him for the very first time in the spring of 1968. And yet . . .

The man who meets me at the door is smiling and friendly. He offers a warm handshake and says how happy he is to meet me.

Paul Brown, then, is easy to get along with. And yet . . .

It is during that first interview. I pose a seemingly innocent question connected with his days as coach of the Cleveland Browns. His smile disappears.

"I know what you're trying to trap me into saying, young man," he says coldly, "and it won't work."

So Paul Brown is a haunted man who refuses to be reminded about the past. And yet . . .

We are walking together in downtown Cincinnati. Jim Brown, author of a book called *Off My Chest,* as well as most of the Cleveland Browns' rushing records, has been in the news lately. Allegedly he hurled his girlfriend from a balcony.

"Did you know Jim Brown has a new book coming out?" Paul Brown asks me. "It's called *Off My Balcony.*"

Paul Brown, therefore, is a good-natured guy. And yet . . .

ABC is getting ready to televise a Monday night game at Riverfront Stadium. But there's one thing the TV people can't figure out. Where are all the signs? Fans always bring cute little signs with cute little sayings and cute little pictures of Howard Cosell to Monday night games.

Paul Brown, the TV people are informed, doesn't allow signs at his home games. They distract from the serious business at hand, he says. People who display signs at football games, he says disdainfully, have "a psychosis to be noticed."

Paul Brown, obviously, is a stuffy man. And yet . . .

It is 1969 and the Bengals are in the middle of the annual college draft. After each choice, Paul Brown informs the assembled press of his team's selection. There is an awkward silence following his announcement of one particular pick. The player in question has an unsavory reputation, rife with allegations of sexual assaults.

"Well," Paul Brown shrugs when this is mentioned, "there's no one on our team he can rape."

Paul Brown apparently, is a tolerant man. And yet . . .

It is 1968. The Bengals, as is Paul Brown's custom, are attending a movie together the night before a game. In the middle of the film, according to his players, Paul Brown stalks out of the theater, calling the show "disgusting." The movie is *Rosemary's Baby.*

Paul Brown, in other words, is a prude, an old-fogey, a sour and humorless man. And yet . . .

It is 1970. I am walking up to the entrance of the staid and dignified Shoreham Hotel in Washington, D.C. Haile Selassie is staying here. And Golda Meir.

Suddenly, a voice calls out. "Hey, Denny." I look around, but see no one. I take another step and the voice comes again. "Hey, Denny." I look around again, bewildered. A third time the voice calls out. And a fourth. Like a dummy I stand in front of this stodgy old hotel, scratching my head.

Finally, high above me on a balcony overlooking the entrance I catch a glimpse of a balding head and a broad smile. Paul Brown is laughing, tickled by his little practical joke. I couldn't have been more surprised if it had been Haile Selassie.

This, then, is Paul Brown: Hard and friendly, haunted and good-natured, stuffy and tolerant. So why did Paul Brown quick-count the sports world with his decision to quit coaching?

Don't ask me. I don't know the man. I never did.

Another Biggest Fight of the Century

June 24, 1976

I see by the sports pages that the annual greatest sports event of all time is upon us once again.

On Saturday, in Tokyo, Mr. Muhammad Ali will confront Mr. Antonio Inoki in a contest of athletic skills the likes of which the world has never seen.

Not that there is anything startling, or even newsworthy, in the fact that Mr. Ali is prepared to fight once again. In recent years, he has appeared in the ring frequently, several times against challengers who did not bleed at the prefight weigh-in.

What makes Saturday's event notable, what separates it from previous sagas of our lifetime, is what can only be termed a marked contrast in styles.

Whereas Mr. Ali is proficient in the noble art of boxing, Mr. Inoki is proficient in the noble art of grunting and groaning.

Mr. Inoki, in short, is a rassler.

A boxer against a rassler. What an idea. And what possibilities it portends for the sporting world. In the future, we can expect to see ice hockey's Canadiens against basketball's Celtics. Chris Evert vs. Secretariat. The Reds against the Bengals, a contest that would doubtless be determined by whether or not the Reds were permitted to use their bats.

Lest anyone think that Saturday's affair has a certain odor to it, an essence of Evel Knievel, an eau de Bobby Riggs, Mr. Ali is quick to point out otherwise. Some $10 million is involved, he notes, and he wouldn't mislead the American public for that kind of money. He neglects to say what kind of money he would mislead the American public for.

Furthermore Mr. Ali has gone on record as saying that he is not fond of Mr. Inoki.

"I don't like Inoki because he talks too much," says Mr. Ali . . . which is something like Jimmy Carter saying that Gerald Ford has too many teeth.

And, as if all of that isn't proof enough of the gravity of this confrontation, Mr. Ali is so concerned that he has hired a tutor to prepare him.

Hiring tutors is an old and honored tradition in the pugilism industry. Mr. Chuck Wepner, known to his friends as the Bayonne Bleeder, hired two former boxers and a Kung Fu master to get him ready for a fight with Mr. Ali last year. Armed with all the knowledge these three gentlemen could impart to him, Mr. Wepner stepped boldly into the ring against Mr. Ali on a cold March night in Cleveland. He was beaten to a pulp.

Mr. Ali's tutor for Saturday's ruckus is Freddie Blassie. Not only is Mr. Blassie a former rassler, he apparently is also an author. According to Mr. Ali, Mr. Blassie "wrote the book on dirt."

In other words, should Mr. Inoki attempt any sneaky maneuvers, Mr. Ali will be prepared to counteract them. By counteract, Mr. Ali explains, he means that he will break both of Mr. Inoki's arms at the elbows.

From Japan, meanwhile, there are no reports that Mr. Inoki has hired a dirty boxer to train him.

According to the latest intelligence, Mr. Inoki is simply trying to toughen his skin so that it will not be pounded into so much sukiyaki. This he is doing by paying persons to walk on his face. It is not yet clear how successful this tactic will be. All that is certain at this point is that Mr. Inoki's dentist is keeping busy.

So there we have it.

In this corner, from Louisville, Ky., carrying a dirty book, Muhammad Ali. And in that corner, with footprints on his face, Antonio Inoki.

"The Martial Arts Championship," for which lots of people are expected to pay lots of money to see at lots of closed circuit television locations.

What's that you say, Mr. Barnum?

Two Men Who Fight

Sept. 30, 1975

It is not, as the newspaper ads suggest, "the saga of our lifetime."

But it is a heavyweight championship boxing match and so, for a day at least, we will all become boxing fans. Just as on the first Saturday in May we all become horse racing fans and every fourth summer we all become political experts.

Therefore, for a day at least, I will become a boxing writer. It is a position for which I am enormously unqualified, except for having met both Muhammad Ali and Joe Frazier, the principals in tonight's "thrilla in Manila."

Both meetings took place in the same week in the same place, last March at a motel in Cleveland, where Ali was lounging in preparation for an upcoming date with a heavy bag named Chuck Wepner.

"If you want an interview, c'mon up to my room tomorrow morning," Ali suggested when I introduced myself to him at a party.

The next morning at 9 I am tapping at his door. A very round man opens it.

"The champ's still in bed," the very round man says. "But you can come in and wait."

Inside, I have a choice. I can watch Merv Griffin on the television or I can stare through the screen that separates the two rooms in the suite to where Ali is in bed with his wife.

Just as I am getting really interested in Merv, Ali appears through the screen. He is wearing a dark blue shirt and slacks and a pair of black work shoes. He speaks briefly with the very round man, then writes him a check.

"He's from Louisville," Ali mentions after the very round man has left. "He's one of them that likes to hang around me because I'm the champ. When I'm not the champ no more, he'll be gone. So will all the others."

He says that matter-of-factly, with a touch of sadness but no rancor. I wonder then why he tolerates them, the leeches, the sycophants, the fawners who call him champ and always have their hands out.

But as we talk — or, rather, as Ali talks and I listen — the question answers itself. In a voice so soft that some of the words do not register on my tape recorder, an Ali emerges that I had never suspected. It is not the bombastic Ali of television, the Ali filled with boasts and rhymes and other things. It is, instead, a reflective and insecure Ali, an Ali worried about what other people think of him and whether or not he will be remembered in history.

Throughout the monologue I am aware of the person in the next room. What do I call her when she joins us? Do I call her Mrs. Ali? Mrs. Muhammad? Mrs. Champ? My concern, it turns out, is groundless. Ali does not bother to introduce her to me and she does not speak. It is just as well, because no matter how I addressed her, I would have been wrong. She is not Mrs. anything. Her name is Veronica Porsche. She is, according to some wire service reports, Ali's cousin.

She sits wordlessly through the remainder of the interview, until finally Ali suggests going down to the coffee shop for breakfast.

"Fine," I say, "I could go for some bacon and eggs."

"Bacon," Ali shouts. "You don't want to eat bacon. Man, that's pork. Don't you know that pork poisons your body? Didn't you ever see a piece of pork with all them worms in it?"

He goes on that way for several minutes, painting a de-appetizing picture of the evils of pork, half joking, half serious. His voice, soft and low during the interview, climbs higher and louder. Muhammad Ali is getting ready to go out in public. It is time for the Muhammad Ali show.

In the elevator, while strangers stare, I ask Ali if he thinks he has slowed down in the past few years. Without warning his fists shoot out in a machine gun flurry of jabs that end less than an inch from my jaw. Six jabs? Ten? Twenty? Who knows how many punches he throws before I can pull back out of danger?

"I am still the fastest . . . the greatest . . . the beautifulest," he crows, throwing me a mock-stern look.

Walking into the coffee shop there is a man standing there, white, middle-aged.

Pete Rose, who knows the answers; Mike Reid, who knows the questions; Paul Brown, whom D.L. doesn't know; Muhammad Ali, who knows when to go public; Whammy Bufano, who knows how to stop you cold; the late Toots Shor, who knew how it used to be; and Soggy the Toad, whose sad saga knows no equal.

"Hello, Mr. Clay," the white man says as Ali walks by.

Behind us, a young black man snarls, "That's Ali. His name is Ali."

But Ali just smiles. "How are you?" he says to the white man.

There is not as much to say about meeting Joe Frazier. He is simply standing there in the lobby, waiting for the obligatory "confrontation" with Ali, the publicity stirrer for a bout that has not yet been announced but which everyone knows is inevitable.

A gorilla is what Ali calls Frazier, and there is a certain amount of truth in that. Although smaller than Ali, Frazier is somehow much more frightening to see.

But he is friendly and smiling when I approach him.

"Glad to meet you," he says. "And who is this?"

"This" is Eric, who is not quite 3 years old and is waiting for daddy to get done asking big men silly questions so he can go swimming in the motel pool.

And fierce, tough, Smokin' Joe Frazier, the former heavyweight champion of the world, bends down to talk to the blond-haired little boy. I don't remember what they talk about, but at the end Joe Frazier is laughing and telling people "that sure is a cute little boy."

A mean sport, boxing. A comment, perhaps, on the values of a society that professes to be revolted at the idea of pitting man against bull and rooster against rooster yet considers it noble when two men stand inside ropes and labor to knock each other into insensibility.

But there is a certain charm to the men who make their livings this way, a charm that makes a heavyweight championship fight something special and makes us all, for a day at least, boxing fans.

And Then There Was Whammy

Mar. 21, 1975
(Winner of 1976 Ohio Associated Press Sports Writing Award)

CLEVELAND—If the Chuck Wepner sideshow didn't exist, Jimmy Breslin would have to invent it. Perhaps he would call it, "The Gang That Couldn't Breathe Straight."

There is Wepner's manager, Al Braverman, whose nose bends to the west. And Paddy Flood, the assistant manager, whose nose bends to the east. They are perfect book ends for Wepner, whose nose doesn't bend at all, but merely spreads across his face like a broken egg in a cold frying pan. "All the cartilage has been removed," Wepner says of his former nose. "Now all that's in there is silly putty."

And there is Two-Ton Tony Galento, who was brought in to teach Wepner how to fight dirtier. And Max Schmeling, who was brought in to teach Wepner something. Possibly German. And a Kung Fu master who reportedly has taught Wepner how to break boards, which will be of enormous value if Muhammad Ali attacks him with a two-by-four Monday night.

Best of all, there is Dominick Bufano who, at the age of 250, still gives the best whammy in Jersey City.

"Wait'll ya see Whammy Bufano," Paddy Flood was saying the other day as we sat in Braverman's hotel room on the outskirts of town. "You're gonna love him. He's got one eye. And two teeth. And when he gives ya the whammy, he scrunches up, like this, and makes this godawful sound."

And Paddy Flood scrunches up until he looks like Charles Laughton playing Quasimodo and makes a sound like a horny rooster.

Whammy Bufano is not here now. He is out somewhere with Chuck Wepner, making a promotional appearance guaranteed to start a stampede of ticket buyers thundering down I-271 to the Richfield Coliseum.

So there is nothing to do right now but listen to Al Braverman recite his list of reasons why Chuck Wepner will not be punched into so many pounds of chopped liver by Ali on Monday. Braverman cites all the big upsets: Braddock over Baer. Clay over Liston. The Jets over the Dolphins. David over Goliath.

"And, jeez, this kid's got heart," Braverman says.

"He's got two hearts," says Flood.

Those who saw his fight against Sonny Liston agree that Wepner has two hearts. One wouldn't have been enough to pump out that much blood.

"The bleeding don't worry us anymore," Braverman insists. "I've got my secret stuff I put on his face about an hour before the fight. It's got Indian herbs in it, and surgeon's paste, and some kind of smelly stuff." Braverman says his secret stuff really works. At least, it works better than the corned-beef brine he once tried.

What Braverman has to say is not nearly as interesting as how he says it. Braverman, an ex-fighter, is a rumpled, harried stereotype of what Hollywood thinks a fight manager should be. He makes full and pungent use of words normally found on latrine walls. Flood, also a one-time fighter, speaks a similar idiom. Sitting between them, it is like being in a pornographic echo chamber.

Eventually, Wepner returns to the hotel. He is accompanied by Whammy Bufano.

"Hey, Whammy, c'mere," Flood says. "I wantcha to meet this guy. He's a writer."

Whammy, who stands only 5-foot-3, including his new green cap, grins shyly and sticks out his hand.

"Naw, not that way," Flood wails. "You know, give it to him."

Whammy stops. He scrunches up. He makes a terrible face. He jabs his fingers at me. He makes a sound like a horny rooster. He looks like Mickey Rooney playing Quasimodo.

It is difficult to know what to ask of an elderly man who says, "Cock-a-doodle-do" to you. It is not, after all, like interviewing Ken Anderson.

"Tell him about your kid brother," Flood suggests.

"Oh, yeah," says Whammy. "He's 91."

"Ninety-one?"

"Yeah."

"Well, how old are you?"

"About 250, near as I can figure."

"Gee, you don't look that old, Whammy. Tell me, who are some of the ones you worked your whammy on?"

"Well, there was Sonny Liston. It worked on him. And that horse, whatsisname . . . oh yeah, Secretariat."

"You think your whammy will work on Ali?"

"Yeah. He ain't got a chance. I give it to him like this."

Scrunch. Jab. Cock-a-doodle-do.

I can feel it working. I'll never be able to write again.

No One Gives a Toot Anymore

July 20, 1976
(Winner of 1977 Ohio Associated Press Sports Writing Award)

NEW YORK—It's all so different now.

Never again will the Babe murder a high, hard one and never again will Casey murder the language. The Dodgers have hit and run to LA and the Giants have skipped to Frisco. Ebbetts Field, the Polo Grounds, the old Madison Square Garden, they're all gone. Graziano is selling hamburgers. DiMaggio is selling coffee pots.

And nobody stops at Toots Shor's anymore.

He's a legend, Toots Shor. A real, honest-to-Damon Runyon, only-in-New York legend. A kid who came from Philly and started as a bouncer and married a Ziegfeld girl and operated taverns that attracted some of the lustiest figures who ever swaggered across a front page.

Toots Shor's restaurants were places where a nobody from Peoria could go and maybe see Hemingway standing at the bar. Or F. Scott Fitzgerald under it. It was a place where he could see the Babe call his shot. Several times a night.

New York without Toots would be Philadelphia, the saying went.

But that's all changed. Now shortstops carry briefcases and quarterbacks wear panty hose and when a nobody from Peoria stops in at Toots Shor's what he sees mostly are other nobodies from Peoria.

Still, there's magic in the name and when I come out of the new Madison Square Garden and see a sign across 33rd Street that says Toots Shor, there is no way I can pass it by. Walk past Toots Shor's? Why, I'd sooner walk past the Louvre.

So I go inside, just to take a look, and before I know it I am sitting at a table with a menu in my hand and a waiter hovering at my left.

This is not the original Toots Shor's, of course. Other places have come before this one, just as there have been other Madison Square Gardens. The newest Toots Shor's is less than a year old and bears the inescapable stamp of Madison Avenue cute. Pictures of sports heroes hang just so on the walls. The menu in my hand is titled, The Scorecard at Dinner. Entrees are listed under the heading, The Heart of the Batting Order.

I order a sirloin for $11.95 from the hovering waiter and while I wait I look around at the pictures that hang just so on the walls. Pictures of O.J. and Billie Jean and Rose and Aaron and a lot of other sports stars who may or may not have come in here.

And in a semi-secluded booth, under a picture of Reggie Jackson, sits 73-year-old Bernard "Toots" Shor.

He is alone, eating his dinner, and I don't really want to interrupt the man in the middle of his meal. But if I don't at least try for an interview, I am no kind of newspaperman at all.

I walk up to where he is sitting and I introduce myself. He is not thrilled to meet me. I can tell he is not thrilled to meet me by the way he says, "Why dontcha go away and leave me alone?"

I start to walk back to my table, because I can take a hint as well as the next guy. But in the next breath he says, "Awww, siddown. But, jeez, not too long, huh? I'm really tired."

So I siddown to talk with 73-year-old Bernard "Toots" Shor and it is like talking with a history book.

He talks about the famous people he has known and the names spill out faster than I can write them down.

He talks about the politicians.

"I've had drinks with eight presidents, starting with Hoover. I'm not braggin'. I'm just tellin' ya."

He talks about the movie stars.

"Hope, Crosby, Gable, Sinatra, they all used to come in."

He talks about the writers.

"See, there used to be eight newspapers in this town and all the writers came in to my place. Hemingway, Fitzgerald, Granny Rice, Bill Corum. And I'll tell ya something else. Every writer paid his check."

That alone makes Toots Shor's unique among taverns in the western world.

But mainly he talks about the athletes.

"I knew them all before they became big stars. The only ones I met after they were stars were Ruth and Dempsey. All the others used to come in long before anybody ever heard of them.

"For years I went to a ball game every day of my life. But Friday nights were the best. There were always fights in the old Garden on Friday nights and all the fighters used to come to my place for lunch at 3 o'clock before their bouts. Jeez, the old

Garden was the greatest place in the world. If I ever wrote a book, I'd call it Friday Night in New York."

The politicians, the movie stars, the writers, the athletes, they don't come in to Toots' place much anymore.

"We don't have anybody come around here today," he said. "Television changed all that. The athletes are different now. They make too much money."

But Toots Shor has no complaints.

"I've got too many memories. Too many wonderful memories," he said. "Let me tellya, if God came down right now and said to me 'What do you wanta be?' I'd tell him, 'A saloon keeper.' What else?"

Soaring Saga of Soggy the Toad

May 24, 1975

VERSAILLES, Ohio — Who knows how far Soggy the toad might have gone?

The times, after all, were perfect for him. Arnie is aging, Bench is struggling, Namath is ailing. Soggy was a toad whose time had come.

His distinctive greenish-brown face would have been known to millions. There would have been commercials ("If our panty hose can make Soggy's legs look good, imagine what they can do for yours"). He would, undoubtedly, have been syndicated. Astronomical fees would have been paid for a share in the world's greatest stud toad.

Broadway Soggy.

But all the hopes, all the dreams, were cruelly crushed yesterday.

Soggy the toad croaked.

There was no hint of the tragedy to come when the Middle School Frog Jumping Contest began yesterday. No warning of the horror that lay ahead.

All seemed normal when Principal Lois Smith signalled for the competition to begin on the asphalt playground.

A record-breaking crowd encircled the track. The entire Middle School student body, the fourth graders from the elementary school, front porch sitters from as far away as across the street.

Were they drawn there by the possibility of death? Or were they merely there because, as one female spectator put it, "I think frogs are cute."

While its fans may deny that they are attracted by it, there is no question that danger is a part of this event.

"One of them got loose and jumped out of a second floor window this morning," Mrs. Smith related. "But he survived. And another one wet all over my desk."

Danger or not, this year's contest drew a huge entry list: 30 toads, 16 bullfrogs, 12 small frogs, two turtles. They came in bait buckets, in coffee cans, in pickle jars, in milk cartons. If they thought of death as they waited for their number to be called, none of them talked about it.

Toad jumping was the first event.

Jupiter, handled by Pam Jutte, brought the first big reaction from the crowd with a hop of six inches. It wasn't, Ms. Jutte lamented, much of a hop. But, at an inch and a half from end to end, Jupiter wasn't much of a toad.

Lila, with the help of a smack on the ground behind her by trainer Richard Williams, soared 23 inches. Two toads later Dale Wilker's Stever the Toad went 27 inches.

Breps Phewf, Teddy the Toad, Racer, Cicero, Berry and Geraldine all tried in vain to match that effort.

Then it was Soggy's turn.

Soggy, like Jupiter, was small. But unlike Jupiter, who came from a well-to-do family in the river, Soggy was a pond toad. And when you grow up in a pond, you grow up tough. Ignoring the scoffs of the crowd, he coiled his small but muscular body, dug his toes into the hot asphalt and hopped.

Did I say hopped? Make it leaped. Nay, make it soared . . . a mighty, majestic arch toward the hot, cloudy sky . . . a blur of greenish-brown against the gray and blue. Hearts stopped, breathing ceased, time stood still as Soggy glided through the air.

There was silence for an instant after he returned to the earth, stunned, awed silence. Then the crowd caught its collective breath and exploded in one long mighty roar, drowning out the official announcement that Soggy had gone 7 feet, 1 inch.

The rest, of course, was anti-climactic. Paul Buscher's Lloyd, the eventual overall champion, won the small frog competition, but his best was only 4-1. Trudy Grogean's Get Lost was the top bullfrog at 6-1, but even that seemed inadequate in comparison with Soggy's noble effort.

If it had ended there this would have been a happy story, an inspiring tale of a glorious deed, and Versailles would be a joyful place today, ready to take its berth alongside Beaver Falls, Pa., and Binger, Okla.

But then came the fateful call announcing the most dangerous of all events, the free-for-all. Ten at a time the contestants were summoned back to the ring, placed in the middle and required to hop out of the circle. The first one out is the winner.

That's when Soggy got it. In the confusion, in the chaos, an unidentified scuffed sneaker flattened him on the ashalt.

For awhile, the shocked crowd was told only that Soggy had a broken leg and that an ambulance was on the way. But all who saw him knew it would be too late. Soggy the toad's next hop would be in that great pond in the sky.

And as he croaked his last, trainer Jim Eilerman voiced the epitaph that will remain forever a part of sport's literature:

"Heck, he's dead."

But surely somewhere in Versailles, the town that gave us Poultry Days, a more comprehensive tribute is even now being penned. Perhaps:

An Ode to a toad

Hear now the saga of Soggy the toad,
A noble creature small and fat.
One moment he soared high to the heavens,
The next moment he went splat.

6 I Spent a Week There One Night

The first trip I ever took as an employee of The Journal Herald was to Augusta, Ga., to cover the Masters Golf Tournament.

When I returned, I figured up my expenses. Despite some of my best creative writing, I found that I had spent 67 cents more than I could account for.

And so I entered on my expense form:

"67 cents . . . for riotous living."

In the business office the next day, two computers and an assistant auditor blew tubes and I was informed that the expense account is no place for levity.

Since then, I have been more circumspect. Whenever I come up with a minor difference in travel expenses, I put down:

"67 cents . . . for entertaining news sources."

Well, Break My Bank!

Feb. 24, 1976

LAS VEGAS — July, 1974. An unidentified big plunger from Texas comes to town. In two days he wins $440,000.

August, 1975. A local man puts $1 into a slot machine at the MGM Grand Hotel and pulls the handle. He wins $152,683.

January, 1976. A high roller from Dayton, Ohio, swaggers into the Circus Circus Hotel-Casino. He wins a green and pink stuffed doggie.

And they say you can't hit it big in Vegas.

But as all of us high rollers are aware, you've got to know what you're doing to break the bank in this town.

First off, you've got to avoid the slots, which lure you with their one-armed salutes exactly 13 steps after you get off your plane at McCarran International Airport. The McCarran slots bring in an annual $1 million. Among airport money-makers around the country, this is second only to the pay toilets at Cox Municipal.

Slot machines are everywhere in Vegas. In casinos, in hotels, in hamburger joints, in gas stations. Well, maybe I shouldn't say that they are everywhere, because I'm not 100 percent sure of that. I didn't visit any churches while I was here.

Anyway, the ubiquitous slots, which swallow anything from pennies to $5 bills, are here mainly for the ubiquitous grey-haired, little old ladies. It is estimated that nine million tourists visit Las Vegas each year. Eight million of them are gray-haired, little old ladies form Peoria.

But the high rollers don't fool around with the forests of slots that grow in Las Vegas. So I ignore the 718 machines in the lobby of the Stardust Hotel as I check in.

I have selected the Stardust for a number of reasons. For its size. For its convenience. For its $9.95 daily room rates during January.

The Stardust contains one of the bigger casinos in town. In addition to the 718 slot machines, it has nine craps tables, 15 poker tables, five roulette wheels, two mini-baccarat tables, 120 keno seats and 41 "21" tables (or is that 21 "41" tables?).

There have been big winners here. And big losers.

"In 1973 I saw a man win $480,000," says Phil Mandel, who oversees the operation of five of the Stardust tables on the 3 to 11 a.m. shift. "He played baccarat, placing $2,000 bets for three straight days.

"On the other side, I saw a man who lost an average of $10,000 a week for three months."

Based on his 11 years of experience, Phil Mandel figures baccarat is the game in which "you have the least going against you."

But then, Phil Mandel adds, "Personally, I don't gamble."

Like Phil Mandel, I don't gamble, either. If Man O' War were alive today, I'd bet him to show. Not even the Stardust sports book, at which you can bet up to $100,000 on the Ohio State-Minnesota basketball game or the fifth at Santa Anita, appeals to me.

Still, you can't come to Las Vegas without trying your luck just once. So I decide to give it one try. But not at the Stardust. After all, they already have my $9.95 and I feel it's only fair to spread my wealth around.

So I head down the Strip to the Circus Circus, which is one of the few casinos you will ever see shaped like a circus tent.

Inside, the circus theme is carried out to extreme. There is the Horse Around Bar, in which you sip your Manhattans while sitting in a merry-go-round. There are the trapeze artists, swinging high above the green, felt tables.

And on the second level there is a carnival-type midway. It is here that I will make my killing. At the booth that says "Guess Your Weight.'

In typical Las Vegas style, there is more than one way to play this traditional midway game. For the really big spenders, there is the three-way parlay. If you wish to press your bet, the girl will guess any three of six categories: Weight, age, years married, home state, month of birth, or occupation.

I decide to shoot the bundle. Casually, I flip my roll on the table. She pockets the $3.

"What do you want me to guess?" she asks.

"Birth month, number of years married and occupation," I

say, just as cool as if I was Jimmy the Greek. I had considered going for home state instead of number of years married, but I figured the Ohio U. sweatshirt I was wearing might tip her off.

She makes her first call.

"You were born in August."

"Wrong," I say. "September."

"You've been married eight years."

"Wrong," I say, "11." (I find out later that we were both wrong. It is 12.)

She has one more chance. If she doesn't guess my occupation, I win. I clean up.

She examines my hands. Inwardly, I groan. What if she sees the paper cuts? The typewriter ribbon stains?

"You are . . . a sales manager."

Jackpot. I have won. All around me I can feel the looks of grudging admiration from the other gamblers as she hands me my payoff, a pink and white checked doggie, with floppy green ears.

Eat your heart out, Amarillo Slim.

On the Sidewalks of New York

July 13, 1976

NEW YORK — This is the saga of Patrick A. Sweeney.

It is a story that is rated "R," containing as it does violence and strong language. There is no sex in this saga, but two out of three ain't bad.

The saga begins late Sunday afternoon when Patrick A. Sweeney, 35, an Ohio state representative from Cleveland and an alternate delegate-at-large to the Democratic convention, walks out of a restaurant on Manhattan's Lower East Side.

His attention is drawn to a green, 1976 Monte Carlo parked at the curb. A man is getting out of the car. He holds a shopping bag in his hand.

Patrick Sweeney watches the scene with more than idle curiosity. The shopping bag belongs to the man. The green car belongs to Patrick Sweeney.

"Hey," Pat Sweeney shouts, "that's my car."

"No, it isn't," the man says.

"The hell it's not," Pat Sweeney roars.

Trapped, the man changes his melody.

"OK, Mister. It's your car. But lemme go, will ya? I never did anything like this before. Here, you can have your stuff back."

He hands the shopping bag to Pat Sweeney, who angrily tosses it aside. Later, Pat Sweeney will learn that the bag contained a $300 camera. His $300 camera.

Being a good citizen, Pat Sweeney decides to detain the man until the proper authorities can be summoned. The man disagrees with this plan. A spirited debate ensues. When the debate concludes, the man has some lumps that he did not have before. At 210 pounds, Pat Sweeney is a very good debater.

In due course, the proper authorities arrive. They see a crowd gathered. They see Pat Sweeney kneeling down. At first, they do not see the man. This is because Pat Sweeney is kneeling on the man's neck.

"You know," says one of the proper authorities to Pat Sweeney, "it would have been a lot better for us if you had finished the job on this guy. It's a lot easier to fill out a DOA report."

Then they take the man away to the proper authority place. He will not be dead on arrival. But he will have knee prints on his neck.

Pat Sweeney is told to report to the Criminal Courts Building in the Bowery at 9:30 yesterday morning to sign an affidavit.

This particular Criminal Courts Building is something of a historical place. It was built by the minions of Boss Tweed, who became famous for patriotism, courage and the imaginative use of numbers. Plaster inside the building, a $20,000 job, wound up costing the city $3 million. If Mr. Tweed were alive today, he would be working on the C5A.

It is doubtful that Pat Sweeney is thinking about all this as he parks his car across the street and goes into the Criminal Courts Building to sign the affidavit.

Twenty minutes later, Pat Sweeney comes out of the Criminal Courts Building, having done his duty as a good citizen. Immediately he notices something about his car. It isn't there.

"What happened to my car?" Pat Sweeney asks.

"It got towed away," he is told. "It was in a no parking zone."

Pat Sweeney goes to the place where they take law-breaking cars. To get his car back, he is told, he must produce $65 for towing charges, $35 for the parking violation and proof of ownership.

Pat Sweeney has $65 for towing charges. He has $35 for the parking violation. He does not have proof of ownership. The car is leased. The papers are in the office of the leasing company. The leasing company is in Lancaster, Ohio.

He explains all this to the cop in charge of returning errant cars. The cop listens. The cop studies Pat Sweeney's identification. The cop says:

"No papers, no car."

Pat Sweeney walks away. All in all, this has not been one of his better visits to New York City. His camera is broken. His car is in jail. He owes the city $100.

Still, it could be worse. He has not been mugged here.

Yet.

And a Catfish at the Base of Her Spine

Feb. 12, 1976

HOUSTON — So I walk into the place and the first thing I see is a hairy little guy with an earring dangling down the left side of his face and the letters L-O-V-E tattooed on his toes. And right away I guess that I am not at a meeting of the Oakwood PTA.

And while I am still trying to figure out why the guy with L-O-V-E on his foot didn't select a five-letter word, like, maybe, W-E-I-R-D, a trim, blonde, young lady wearing glasses and a black dress walks up to me and asks if I'd like to see her catfish.

Before I can explain to her that catfish are more in Jim Robey's line, she turns her back and hikes up her skirt and, sure enough, there is a catfish tattooed at the base of her spine.

All of which is not exactly what I had expected when I flew here to witness the first World Convention of Tattoo Artists and Fans.

Somehow I was thinking more along the lines of a roomful of sailors, with crossed anchors on their muscular forearms and parrots perched on their knotty shoulders. And they'd all be bow-legged (the sailors, that is) and say things like, "Ahoy, matey" and "Yo-ho-ho." And when they took their shirts off you'd see that they had a picture of the Constitution sailing across their chests.

As a matter of fact, there are some sailors among the more than 100 tattoo artists who have gathered for the convention at the downtown Holiday Inn. There is 65-year-old Sailor Sid out of Miami, for instance. But when Sailor Sid takes off his shirt there is a golden ring hanging from just about the spot where the poop deck of the Constitution should have been.

"Naw, it didn't hurt a bit," Sailor Sid scoffs when you ask him if it isn't just a tiny bit painful to have one's nipple pierced. "They just put ice on it for about 10 minutes beforehand."

Sailor Sid used to wear two golden rings, but one night the other one got caught in a blanket while he was sleeping and it tore off.

"Now *that* hurts," Sailor Sid admits. "But puttin' them in don't hurt none. Ask my wife here, she's got 'em, too."

Mrs. Sid shakes her head to indicate that it really don't hurt none. But she does not offer to display her golden rings.

Anyway, I did not come here to study golden rings. I came here to see tattoos. So I leave Mr. and Mrs. Sid with their rings dangling and stroll about the crowded meeting room to see what's happening in the skin game.

The thing you have to realize is that just about all tattoers also are tattooees, walking Blinn boards for their craft.

Like Peter Poulos, a muscular 29-year-old tattoo studio owner from Denver, who displays a mostly blue arm that he estimates carries 80 tattoos on it.

Peter Poulos charges $1.50 a minute and he is, I gather, very accomplished in his field. There are whistles of admiration from his peers when he shows them a four-color rose he has inscribed on the calf of a young lady named Barbara. At least, I assume the whistles are for the rose.

Not having a trained eye for such matters, the thousands of tattoos walking around the room strike me as having an overwhelming sameness, a blue parade of snakes and birds and fish and flowers. There doesn't seem to be anything really unique here.

Not like the man I read about who had his last will and testament engraved on his back. Or the aging gent who retaliated against his failing memory by having his name and address tattooed on him. Or the woman who advertised her libbish tendencies with the tattooed motto: "Death before dishwashing."

But if the art here is not extraordinary, the artists themselves certainly are.

Take Lyle Tuttle of San Francisco, the winner of the first beauty contest for tattooed persons, who walks on the stage in a lacy-blue body suit and a pair of brown and white shorts. Only when you look closer you see that the brown and white shorts are all that he is wearing.

The lacy-blue body suit is a series of tattoos that starts at the base of his neck and continues uninterrupted all the way down to his ankles. And if you ask him, he will prove to you that the series really is uninterrupted.

There is 22-year-old Kim Schweers of Lincoln, Neb., one of the growing number of female artists, who carries a rainbow on her shoulder and tells people that she is "the pot of gold at the end of the rainbow." She also wears a rose on her hip, which she says is a good conversation starter.

And there is Valeria Dare, the only black tattoo artist on the scene, who wins the female division of the beauty contest, even though the tattoos don't really show up very well on her dark skin. Val, who says she has a studio in Binghamton, N.Y., and a master's degree from Columbia, carries a number of Hebrew letters engraved on her body. Her husband wears Nazi swastikas.

And there is, most of all, Elizabeth Weinziri of Portland, Ore., who has white hair and a blue polka-dot dress and looks like everybody's grandmother.

When the beauty contest has ended, the guy on the microphone asks Elizabeth Weinziri how come she didn't enter and she giggles and blushes and says, "Oh goodness, nobody wants to look at me with all those pretty young things around." But the guy with the microphone coaxes her to come up and finally she does, looking all embarrassed while people take pictures of her tattooed leg below the hem of her polka-dot dress.

Then someone shouts out, "Show us the rest of them, Elizabeth." And the next thing you know gray-haired little old Elizabeth Weinziri has her back to the audience and she is holding the blue polka-dot dress up around her shoulders so that everyone can see her tattoos and her panty hose and her bra strap and her wrinkles.

I think I liked the guy with L-O-V-E on his toes better.

Not One Blessed Stomp or Whoop

Feb. 10, 1976

NASHVILLE — First, I find out that Minnie Pearl's real name is Sarah Ophelia Colley and she graduated from Ward Belmont College, one of those fashionable girls' finishing schools. Which is OK, I guess, because I didn't really figure she spent her whole life walking around wearing a hat with the price tag dangling from it.

Then I find out that just about the time Tammy Wynette was writing "Stand By Your Man," she was getting a divorce so she could marry George Jones. And that's okay, too, because maybe she meant to call the song "Stand By Your Men."

But then I go to my first Grand Ole Opry, all set for a good ol' night of stompin' and hootin' and real down-home hollerin', and what I find is about 3,000 folks sitting around real quiet, like they were watching open heart surgery. Not one blessed stomp. Not even a single whoop. Heck, I've seen people having more fun than this in a dentist's waiting room.

So I head backstage, where all the performers are standing around talking and sipping lemonade and waiting for their turn to go on and I look for someone to ask about this.

Which is a problem in itself, because I'm really not too familiar with country music stars. I figure I would probably recognize Johnny Cash, but that's easy. He's the one who's always dressed in black and walks around saying, "Hello, I'm Johnny Cash." And if Dolly Parton was walking down one of the narrow hallways that connect the dressing rooms, I'm sure

I'd notice her. I mean, how're you gonna miss Dolly Parton in a narrow hallway?

But Johnny isn't here. And if Dolly's around, I haven't bumped into her. And all the rest of them sort of look alike to me in their mod cowboy suits and their long dresses. It's not like walking into a sports locker room, where all the players wear numbers so you can tell Pete Rose from Joe Morgan.

So for a long time I just stand there, riffling through my $3 Grand Ole Opry program, trying to match the pictures with the faces here in the artists' lounge. Finally I match a picture with a face and I walk up to Connie Smith and ask her why the audience is so quiet.

"It's like when you move into a new house," she says. "You know, the kids sort of tiptoe around for awhile until they get used to it and start feeling comfortable."

Which is probably true. After 31 years at the old Ryman Auditorium, the Opry moved into this brand-new building in March of '74. And a real nice place it is, with its air conditioning and soft red seats and modern acoustics. And the whole thing sits in the middle of a sparkling new place called Opryland U.S.A., which the souvenir program calls a "family entertainment center," although if I didn't know better I'd call it an amusement park.

Some of the Opry performers are glad of the move.

"I love working here," says Lester Flatt. "In the old place you'd burn in the summer and freeze in the winter."

Flatt, who has been working the Opry since 1944, which was even before he met Earl Scruggs, talks on for awhile. He recalls how Opry performers, no matter how big they were, got $7 a show. Now they get $60 for each of the 20 shows they are required to participate in here during the year. It's like being on the *Tonight Show.* You do it for the exposure, not for the money.

Then Lester Flatt says he has to get going, so I thank him and begin to wander around backstage. The next thing I know I am standing on the stage. Not near the stage. Not in the wings. But ON the stage, maybe 10 feet from where Roy Acuff is singing into the microphone that carries his voice to the 3,000 persons in the audience and the unseen millions who are listening to him on their radios.

But no one seems to notice, or care, that I am standing there. This is the way the Opry has always been. Loose. Easy. People with no apparent function standing around on the stage. Kids darting between the microphones. Folks not letting the singers interrupt their conversations.

On the stage, then, it is still the same as it always was. Only the audience seems to have changed.

"In the old place the audience gave you a real high," says Skeeter Davis as she walks off the stage after her song. "I keep waiting for the high to come here, but it never does. The old place seemed to have so much more soul."

"The crowd here is hard to entertain because you're in competition with the building," agrees Sonny Osborne of the Osborne Brothers, who grew up in Dayton and went to school in Jefferson Twp. "What this place needs is somebody to take their instrument and beat it against the wall. Mark it up a little. Take the newness out."

Then Sonny and Bobby Osborne, "The Fastest Grass Alive," step up to the microphone, leaving me to stand there alone again on the stage. I listen for awhile, looking out at the crowd that is sitting on its hands.

It has been a day of disillusionment. Minnie Pearl a finishing school product. Tammy Wynette not standing by her man. An Opry crowd that does not hoot and stomp.

I decide to leave before someone comes up and tells me that Grandpa Jones went to Harvard.

Doing the Air Midwest Shuffle

Mar. 2, 1976

DODGE CITY, Kan. — Now I know why the cowboys always drive their cattle into Dodge City. Flying in would have made 'em loco.

I mean, they told me that Air Midwest was a little outfit. But nobody mentioned that whoever draws the short straw has to leave his suitcase behind.

But maybe I'd better start at the beginning, which is in Wichita, where I am waiting to board Air Midwest flight 905, direct to Dodge City, with intermediate stops at Great Bend and Hutchinson.

It is only 10 minutes to the scheduled departure, but apparently there has been a delay, because no Air Midwest planes can be seen through the large windows that overlook Gate 9.

Idly, I wander to the end of the concourse and look out the small window there, to where a college-aged kid in a plaid sport shirt is putting some things into the nose of a little twin-engine plane.

Something strikes me about the scene. There is something familiar down there. Something I've seen before. Something . . . hey, wait a minute! That's my suitcase.

Hey, kid, hold on. You're putting my suitcase on that little tiny plane and I'm supposed to be flying on Air Midwest 905 and . . . oh, jeez, that IS Air Midwest 905.

Of course, the kid can't hear me moaning. And, anyway, he's got problems of his own.

After he gets my suitcase into the hole in the nose of the plane, he's still got two mail bags, a briefcase, a duffel bag, a large crate and another suitcase left.

He puts in the other suitcase. But then he can't get the duffel bag in. He takes out the mail bags. And the briefcase. He puts in the duffel bag. With some might, he also wedges in the suitcase.

Everything's OK, except now the mail bags aren't in. He takes out the suitcase. He jams in the mail bags. He closes the door and says the hell with it.

When next we see the suitcase, it is inside the terminal, where the gate agent is explaining to its owner that he has a choice. Either he can get on the plane, or his suitcase can. There isn't enough room for both of them.

The man, who is a salesman bound for Hutchinson, decides he can probably make more contacts there than his suitcase can. His suitcase will be sent on the 9 p.m. bus to Hutchinson.

At last we are ready to board. The plane is a Cessna 402, which comes equipped with 10 seats and a *Field and Stream* magazine. The first passenger who gets on automatically becomes the co-pilot. I am the last to board, so I sit in the back seat. Before I can get comfortable, I am told that I can't sit there.

Why not?

Because if there's too much weight in the back, the tail won't get off the ground. I volunteer to move up.

Sitting in a plane where you can see everything is a mixed blessing. On the one hand, it's comforting to be able to see the fuel gauge and know there really is fuel in the tanks. On the other hand, it's disconcerting to see the pilot reading what appears to be an instruction manual as we taxi to the runway.

"You learning how?" one of the passengers asks the pilot.

"Yep. It's all right here, step by step. It looks pretty easy to me."

Apparently he is a quick study, because the take-off is perfect and the flight to Hutchinson is smooth. Even at only 170 miles an hour it takes just 15 minutes to reach Hutchinson Municipal Airport, also known as Hap Stevens Field.

When we have wheeled up to the terminal gate, the pilot tells us we must all disembark while the plane is refueled. Quickly, I head for the terminal, before he says we have to chip in for gas.

The terminal is small, but not without its attractions. Over the Dr. Pepper machine, for instance, hangs a mounted blue marlin, landed by Harry Tidd on July 19, 1949. Harry Tidd, I assume, hails from Hutchinson. The fish, I assume, does not.

In the middle of the terminal is a 3,000-pound piece of rock salt, which is something that LaGuardia doesn't have.

The nicest thing about small terminals like this one is that you don't have to fool around with security checks and metal detectors. Apparently no one is concerned about skyjackers at this field. But then, so what if a skyjacker did get aboard? Where's he gonna force the pilot to fly to? Emporia?

When the refueling is finished, we all get back on the plane. All except the salesman who has business in Hutchinson. He is walking briskly out into the parking lot.

Of course, it's easy to walk briskly when you don't have a big suitcase to carry.

It's a Saga, Plain(s) and Simple

May 12, 1977

PLAINS, Ga. — A brief history of Plains, some of which is factual:

Plains is located in Sumter County, which is in the southwest section of Georgia. The nearest large city is Columbus, Ga., which is best known for being across the river from Phenix City, Ala.

The area surrounding Plains originally was inhabited by Creek Indians, a proud people who lived by hunting, growing corn and fishing the bountiful waters of the Chattahoochee and Pahdel rivers.

In 1827, the Creeks were forced to leave their native land under the Treaty of Washington, also known as the Doctrine of Manifest Urban Renewal.

With the Indians gone, settlers streamed into the area. But life was not nearly as easy for them as they had expected it to be. The Pahdel River, for instance, proved to be treacherous for those unfamiliar with its meandering ways.

Without the Indians to guide them, settlers' boats frequently became grounded on sandbars, or snagged by hidden tree roots. For years the settlers struggled with the problem of being up the Pahdel without a Creek.

In 1885, the Americus, Preston and Lumpkin Railroad came into Sumter County. But the tracks did not extend to Plains, much to the distress of the city fathers.

The city fathers pleaded with the railroad officials to bring the railroad to Plains. But the railroad officials turned a deaf ear. Many railroad officials have deaf ears. It is the result of listening to too many train whistles.

Unable to convince the railroad to come to Plains, Plains went to the railroad. The entire town — lock, stock and cotton gin — moved to Plains' present location.

It was an impressive achievement for the city fathers. But it was just another pain in the bustle for the city mothers, because they were the ones who got stuck with all the packing and unpacking.

It was at this time that the name of the town was changed.

The original name actually was the Plains of Dura, a reference to the Bible story about Nebuchadnezzar and the fiery furnace.

The name was shortened to Plains at the suggestion of a forward-looking city father who realized that "Plains of Dura Baptist Church Bars Blacks" would make a cumbersome headline.

Early in the 20th century, Plains grew rapidly. By 1919 it was a thriving agricultural settlement and a major shipper of cattle and hogs. Still, the basic nature of the town remained conservative. As late as 1924, the town's only streetwalker was a virgin.

The Carters are one of the best known families in Plains. Nearly everyone in town has heard of them. Of course, Carter family members are easy to recognize. They're the ones with the sunburned teeth.

The Carter family has always been important in this part of the state, starting with Wiley Carter, who moved to Sumter County in 1851, shortly after he invented the peanut.

Wiley Carter was the great-great-grandfather of the President. He died in 1864. There is little evidence to indicate that he spent much time with Jimmy.

In spite of what many Republicans think, Jimmy Carter's father and mother were married in 1923.

When she was not otherwise occupied in cooking, cleaning, sewing and inventing white hair, Bessie Lillian Gordy Carter gave birth to four children.

The oldest is Jimmy, who left town to find work shortly after he invented telling the truth. The youngest is Billy. He invented gas stations.

The other two are Ruth, who is an evangelist, and Gloria, who is a trivia question.

On Saturday, we will study Plains, Ga., as it is today.

We will stop at Cousin Hugh Carter's antique store and talk with him about worms.

We will stop at the Plains Realty Co. and talk about land that costs $11 an inch.

We will stop at Billy's cruddy Amoco station and drink a beer.

Will the residents of quiet little Plains be happy to see us loud-mouth, pushy Yankees?

Of course they will. We will bring lots of money.

Plains Just Goes Nuts over Jimmy

May 14, 1977

PLAINS, Ga. — Just because I happen to be in Georgia does not mean I have to visit Plains. Heck, I don't even like Pabst.

On the other hand, I figure if I time it right, I could be the millionth reporter to visit the town where the First Brother lives. They might present me with a gold typewriter. The key to the city. The key to Billy's rest room.

So I fly from Atlanta to Columbus, Ga., a 48-minute trip — 18 minutes in the air, 30 minutes on the runway. At the Columbus airport I go to the Budget Rent-A-Car desk. I get a compact that comes equipped with air conditioning, AM-FM stereo and cleverly hidden gas charges.

The drive from Columbus to Plains via U.S. 280 takes an hour and a half. After 58 miles of pine trees, red dirt and RC Cola signs, I reach the center of Plains (pop. 683). It's easy to tell when you are in the center of Plains. That's where the traffic signal is.

The main street in Plains is called Main Street. It looks a great deal like what Hollywood thinks the main street of a small southern or western town should look like. Half a dozen stores clustered together . . . an overhang protecting the sidewalk . . . a lazy dog lying in the shade, waiting for a quick brown fox to jump over it.

The stores have separate owners and sell different items, but they have two things in common:

They all carry Carter souvenirs — Amy Carter coloring books, Jimmy Carter records, Billy Carter T-shirts. And they all display peanut products — raw, roasted, candied; peanut brittle, peanut oil, peanut cookbooks. And don't forget to try Just Plains Peanut ice cream.

I stop first at Carter's Antiques, which is run by Hugh Carter Sr., Jimmy's first cousin. The First First Cousin is in the back of the store.

"Jimmy used to work right here in this store," Hugh Carter

Sr. says. "Now my boy, Hugh Jr., he's about your age, works for him in Washington."

Hugh Carter Sr. is a Georgia state senator. In addition to the antique store, he operates a worm farm which he thinks may be the largest in the world. He handles 15 million worms a year. Which means he has to wash his hands a lot.

Hugh Carter Sr. says stories about locals resenting the flood of tourists and newsmen that have inundated Plains are mostly untrue.

"A few people have moved," he admits. "But it's been good for the town mainly. I know my business here has doubled. They say in the next 12 months, we'll have 1,800,000 coming in."

Hugh Carter Sr. says he doesn't think Plains will ever again be an anonymous little town.

"It's here forever," he says. "Johnson City, where LBJ lived, is still getting 2,000 a month. Heck, people still go to Warm Springs."

Hugh Carter Sr. seems content to talk about tourists and worms all afternoon, but I have other things to see. I thank him for his time and walk out of the store.

"If you're ever in Washington," he calls after me, "stop by and see my boy at the White House. He'll be glad to see you. Just go to the West Wing and tell him I said to look him up."

I walk along Main Street, past the Peanut Museum with its peanut machine and its peanut movie, until I see the Plains Realty Co. The Plains Realty Co. does not sell peanut pie, peanut pizzas or peanut pop. But it does sell "mini-peanut plantations."

"How big is a mini-peanut plantation?" I ask the man in the realty office.

"One square inch," he says.

"One inch? That's ridiculous. Who would have a tractor that small?"

"Oh, it's just for conversation," he says. "For $11 we sell you a certificate showing that you own one inch of land that used to belong to Jimmy Carter. For an extra $10 we'll sell you a frame. We've sold a lot of them already. Car dealers and other real estate companies buy them to use in their promotions. It's just for laughs."

Doing most of the laughing is an Atlantan named David Thurmond, who is selling the plantations. An acre, I am told, contains 6,272,640 square inches. David Thurmond owns 5 acres. That's 31,363,200 square inches. Or $344,995,200.

I leave the Plains Realty Co. and cross Main Street to Church Street. I pass the Plains Tour Service, which charges $2.50 to take you for a tour of the town on the "Peanut Special" mini-train.

Then I am at the world's most famous gas station.

Billy Carter's Amoco station has not let fame go to its head. The inside of the station is just as unappealing as all the stories have made it sound. A sofa and chair with matching gashes flank a green plastic garbage can. Atlas air filters decorate one wall. A Farrah Fawcett poster stares pointedly down on the scene from another. A row of coolers keeps the Blue Ribbon cold.

Billy is not here.

"Lately he comes in about every afternoon for 5 or 6 minutes," a college-age employe says. "Mainly he just talks to his friends and then leaves. Don't know what time he'll be in today."

As I sit on the gashed sofa, nursing a beer and munching on peanuts, two matronly women walk in. They are wearing matronly white shoes and matronly flowered dresses. Their hair is matron blue. They are, I learn, part of a bus tour from Atlanta, and this is one of their big stops.

They go to the coolers, take out a couple of Blue Ribbons and pop the tops. In the middle of the grimy, cluttered gas station, the two matronly, blue-haired women suck down their beers. From the cans. The scene is unreal.

It is time to leave. I walk through the oppressive heat, which is in the mid-90's now, until I come to my rented car, the one with the air conditioning, AM-FM stereo and hidden charges.

Just as I am about to get in, I notice something on the bottom of my shoe. It is brown and squishy . . . I take a stick and scrape it off. It is just as I feared.

Peanut butter.

Let's Hear It for the Bull

Mar. 5, 1977

MEXICO CITY — On a midwinter Sunday afternoon, the place to be in Mexico City is at the bullring.

Being in Mexico in the winter and not going to a bullfight is unthinkable. It is like being in downtown Dayton at night and not getting propositioned.

So at 3 o'clock on a warm Sunday afternoon, I am in a cab headed for the Plaza Mexico, the No. 1 bullring in the country.

The program does not begin until 4:30, but I have to get there early, because the ticket promised by my travel agency, Titanic Tours, has failed to materialize.

As we weave through the heavy traffic on Calz. San Antonio, I ask the cabbie how difficult it will be to get a ticket today.

He shrugs and blows his horn at a Renault he has just forced off the road.

"Normally, it would not be difficult," he says, swerving just in time to keep a bus from getting past us. "But this is the inauguracion. The first fight of the season."

"Oh, wow, sort of like Opening Day in baseball."

Si, he says, giving a blast of his horn to a pedestrian crossing the street in front of us. While the cabbie leans on the horn and the pedestrian shakes his white cane at us, I sit back and consider the odds.

I have not had much experience with scalpers, especially in a foreign language. I don't even know how to say, "Psst, hey buddy," in Spanish.

In addition to which, I have no idea what a bullfight ticket looks like. I'm liable to shell out a couple of hundred pesos for a ticket entitling me to a free lube job with my next fill-up.

On the positive side, I have plenty of money in my pocket and the company's blessing to spend it. I think back to what they told me before I left the office.

"As long as you get a good bullfight story, we don't care what it costs," assignments editor Finster "Hi Roller" O'Shaughnessy declared. "Go as high as 10 bucks if you have to."

Then we are as near to the Plaza Mexico as the snarled traffic will permit. I hop out of the cab and pay the fare, which is 100 pesos. (The same ride back to my hotel after the fights will cost me 50 pesos. This is just one of the things that makes Mexico a land of mystery).

Semi-confidently I join the flow of one-way pedestrian traffic moving towards the stadium, until I am standing in the middle of Calle Augusto Rodin, the street that runs in front of Plaza Mexico.

The area is crammed with people. There are old people and young people, tall people and short people, fat people and skinny people. But they all have one thing in common.

Not a one of them has an extra ticket.

For a while, I just stand around, waiting for a scalper to approach me. At 3:30 I still have hopes of buying a good seat in the sombra, the shady side of the ring. By 3:45, I am willing to take a seat in the sun. By 4 p.m., I am willing to sit next to the bull.

Perhaps I am being too subtle, I think. Maybe I should do something that will make it plain what I want. Like taping a $20 bill to my forehead.

At 4:10, a middle-aged man approaches me.

"Do you need a ticket?" he asks, in lightly-accented English.

"Maybe. How much?"

"One hundred pesos."

I do some lightning quick mental math. It's 20 pesos to the dollar. Or is that 20 dollars to the peso! If it's 20 pesos to the dollar, that'll be $5. On the other hand, if its 20 dollars to . . .

"I don't have all day, senor."

"Oh, sorry. OK, let me see the ticket."

He produces a pink and violet ticket with a picture of a man on a horse being chased by a bull. It's a bullfight ticket, all right. Either that or a ticket for a John Wayne movie. The price on the ticket is 45 pesos.

"OK," I say. I give the man his money.

"Follow me," he says.

Then I am inside the famed Plaza Mexico, the world's biggest bullring. As we walk to our seats, the man who sold me the ticket says that his name is Rodolfo Vasquez and he is an accountant who has traveled extensively in the United States.

Each year, he says he buys two season tickets for himself and his wife. But his wife is sick this week and so Rodolfo Vasquez is doing what any red-blooded Mexican bullfight fan would do: He is going without her.

Our seats are in the sombra, high up in the lower deck. We reach them at precisely 4:30. Just as we sit down, there is a flourish of trumpets from somewhere in the stands above us.

It is the signal to begin the corrida, the running of the bulls.

At the opposite side of the ring a gate opens and the procession begins. This is what I have been waiting to see. The pageantry. The color. The spectacle.

The alguaciles, horsemen in 16th century costumes, come first. They are followed by the picadors, the banderilleros, the matadors. Everyone is in the parade but the bulls. In bullfighting, only the home team gets introduced.

I snap a couple of pictures and look down to adjust my camera. When I look up, the ring is empty again. I glance at my watch. It is 4:35. The pageantry, the color, the spectacle I have been hearing so much about takes just five minutes.

I have seen better ceremonies at the opening of a Burger Chef.

And then the first bull is in the ring, running, snorting, in search of an enemy. He finds many.

There are the picadors on their well-padded horses, who drive their lances into the large muscle at the back of his neck.

There are the banderilleros, agile men who plunge barbed staves into the wound to increase the flow of blood.

There are not one but three matadors, calling to him, taunting him, bewildering him, forcing him to run around the ring so that his heart will pump faster and the blood will flow more freely.

And then, when he is worn, weakened by the loss of blood, unable to hold up his head, unable to keep his tongue from dragging in the dust of the ring, one matador comes forth to challenge him.

Sometimes, it is said, a bull can win his life with an exceptional show of bravery. It does happen. About once every 50 years.

But the fight is almost always fixed. They wouldn't touch it in Vegas. Even a bull that defeats his final tormentor winds up being slaughtered, his meat given to the poor or sold right there at the bullring.

I sit through three fights, trying to understand what is happening down there, looking for the beauty that Hemingway found in the sight of men tormenting dumb animals.

But I am no Hemingway.

I see no beauty down there. I see only a depressing reminder of how little my species has progressed.

After the third killing, the one in which the matador slides his sword deep into the animal's back, puncturing a lung and causing gushers of blood to pump out the bull's nose and mouth, I decide that I have had enough.

The program is only half over. The best fights are yet to come. The bravest bulls. The greatest macho.

Yet to come, too, is a tragic bit of foolishness when a young man vaults from the stands into the ring during the sixth fight and is badly gored. This, I learn, is becoming a tradition at bullfights. The flamboyant El Cordobes got his start that way, according to the legend.

But when the young man jumps into the ring at Plaza Mexico, I am no longer in my seat. I am wandering outside, sorting through the souvenirs, sampling the foods for sale at the booths that stand temporarily in the shadow of the stadium.

I doubt that I will ever return to Plaza Mexico. Or to any bullring.

It is not that I am bothered by the blood, although Lord knows there is plenty of that. Nor does the sight of a dead animal upset me. I enjoy steak as much as the next guy.

But, if you're going to kill an animal, get it over with. Shoot it. Hang it. Blow its head off with a bazooka.

But don't bleed it and torment it and wait until it is wild-eyed with fear and confusion while you do it. Don't spend 20 minutes torturing an animal and then tell me about your macho.

That's not macho. That's only another way of pulling the wings off of flies.

A Hot Time in the Old Town

Mar. 3, 1977

MEXICO CITY — It's not as if I am unfamiliar with Mexican cuisine.

Nacho cheese tortilla chips. Jalapena bean dip. Taco Bell. Gold Star Chili. You name it, I've tried it.

Still, I am somewhat unsure of myself as I enter the Fonda El Pato for my first restaurant meal in Mexico.

The Fonda El Pato (which means Inn of the Duck), is not one of those tourist restaurants where they put a chili pepper on top of the prime rib and mold the Jello into the shape of a sombrero.

It is a real, authentic Mexican restaurant, where real, authentic Mexicans eat. I can tell it is a real, authentic Mexican restaurant because the BankAmericard sign on the window is in Spanish.

Inside, a waiter shows me to a table and waits to take my drink order. This is my big chance. I have been practicing my Spanish for weeks, planning for this very moment.

"Cerveza, por favor," I say, just as smooth and suave as Ricardo Montalban.

A few minutes later he brings my beer.

"Gracias," I say. The waiter nods. It is obvious he is dazzled by my flawless command of the language.

Each time he approaches after that, I give him the "cerveza, por favor," routine. After the fourth "cerveza, por favor," I realize there is one major flaw in my planning. When I was learning the word for "beer," I neglected to learn the word for "men's room."

With the help of a little sign language, and a great deal of dancing up and down, I convey my needs to the waiter. He points me in the right direction.

When I return to the table a few minutes later, my image as a cosmopolitan sophisticate is shot. But I feel a lot better.

I decide to order.

I start with "Sopa de Tortilla Seca (al horno con queso)," which costs 28 pesos. I'm not sure I will like it, but it looks like a real bargain to me at less than a peso a letter.

To follow the tortilla soup, I order the "Plato Mexicano," which includes: Filete, enchilade de mole, quesadilla, two flautas and chalupa y frijoles.

The entire platter costs just 63 pesos ($3.15). On the other hand, I have no idea what any of it is.

When the waiter returns, he is carrying a small metal bowl of greenish stuff and a wooden spoon. Eagerly, I try a spoonful of the greenish stuff. It is, I am surprised to discover, cold.

At least, it is cold until it hits the back of my tongue. Then it is hot.

Not "oh-my-goodness-that-is-rather-spicy" hot.

The kind of hot I'm talking is "oh-my-God-call-the-fire-department-Clara-it's-a-triple-three-alarm" hot.

After I choke down the first spoonful, I look around to see if anyone has noticed my reaction. But no one is paying any attention. In this restaurant, apparently they are used to the sight of grown men crying.

I try a few more spoonfuls, but it is no use. I can't finish it. Eating that stuff is like being burned at the stake from the inside.

Eventually, the waiter returns. This time, he is carrying a plate of something. It looks like shredded coconut on a bed of noodles. It is delicious.

Just as I finish the last bite, the waiter reappears. This time he is carrying a large platter.

"Plato Mexicano," he says, putting it down in front of me.

"Plato Mexicano?" I repeat. "But I just finished a Plato Mexicano."

"Oh, no, Senor. That was the sopa tortilla."

"Wait a minute. If that stuff on the plate was sopa tortilla, what the heck is this stuff in the metal bowl?"

"That, senor? That is the hot sauce."

"Hot sauce? I thought it was the soup. I ate half of it."

Laughing, the waiter walks away. He stops to talk to another waiter. I cannot understand what they are saying, but it is obvious they are talking about me.

I can tell they are talking about me, because every once in awhile I hear the phrase:

"El stupido."

Disconnected by Mamacita Bell

Mar. 12, 1977

TAXCO, Mexico — "Hello, front desk, I want to call the woman who promised to love, honor and stuff my tortillas."

"Que?"

"Oh, sorry. I mean, I'd like to place a long distance phone call."

"Si. Uno momento."

"Hello, senor, this is the No-Surprises Inn operator. What is it you wish?"

"I wish to place a phone call to the United States."

"To where do you wish to call"

"To Dayton, Ohio."

"*Day*-tohn? Will you spell that please, senor?"

"Certainly. That's D-A . . ."

"Aye?"

"No, no. 'A.' As in, uh, adios."

"Adios, senor."

★ ★ ★

"Hello, front desk? I had a little problem there. See, I was spelling Dayton for the operator and when I said 'A' as in 'adios' she thought I meant goodby and so she hung up, but I still want to place the call."

"Que?"

"Operator, por favor."

"Si."

"Yes, senor, this is the operator. What is it you wish?"

"I wish to try that phone call again."

"Si, senor. Where is it that you wish to call?"

"Dayton, Ohio. In the United States."

"Day-tohn? Will you spell that, please?"

"That's D-A as in, uh Aztec, T . . ."

"Cee?"

"No, not 'cee.' Tee. Tee. Tee, as in take your telephone and . . ."

"It is not necessary to shout, senor. The connection is quite good."

"You're right. I'm sorry. Look, operator, let's forget the name of the city. All you really need is the area code and the number, anyway."

"Si, senor."

"OK. The area code is 513."

"One moment and I will connect you."

"No, wait a minute, operator. That's only the number of the area code. You still don't have the phone number."

"What is the number?"

"OK. That's 513 . . ."

"513-513?"

"No, just one 513."

"Your number is 1-513?"

"Oh, good grief. Listen, operator, let's just start again, all right? Just forget everything I said."

"Si, senor. What is it you wish?"

"I wish to place a long distance phone call. The number is 513-429-0335. Got that?"

"Of course, senor. I will ring your room when the call is through. It will be perhaps 10 minutes."

"Muchas gracias."

"You're welcome."

"Senor Stewart? This is the hotel operator."

"Boy, it's about time. You said 10 minutes, and it's been way over an hour."

"I am very sorry, senor. I have been trying the entire time, but I have not been able to put through your call."

"Can't put it through? Whaddya mean you can't put it through? Listen, I promised her before I left that I was going to call her tonight and if she doesn't hear from me she's going to be very upset. I mean, if I forget to call her when I'm just going to be late for dinner, it's worth a week on the couch. Do you realize what's going to happen if she doesn't hear from me tonight? I might as well become a monk."

"I am very sorry, senor. There is nothing I can do. The line must be down between here and Mexico City."

"Well that's just great. I'll tell you one thing: If I wind up divorced, I'm naming your crummy phone company as co-respondent."

"Si, senor. Oh, one more thing, senor. When you check out in the morning, you will notice a 15-peso charge."

"15 pesos. That's 75 cents. What for?"

"Phone service, senor."

The (Thr)ill of Deep Sea Fishing

Mar. 17, 1977

ACAPULCO, Mexico — A colorful sport, deep sea fishing.

The azure of the afternoon sky. The sapphire of the gently rolling ocean. The bright orange trim of the sturdy boat. The pale green of my face.

Incredibly enough, the thought of seasickness never crosses my mind when I decide that this is the place to make my debut as a deep sea fisherman.

All I can think of is the action, the excitement. Curt Gowdy battling a sailfish. Julius Boros reeling in an amberjack. Ahab and the white whale. The old man and the sea. The Captain and Tennille.

And so at 6 a.m., with the sky still black over Acapulco Bay, I crawl from my bed and take a cab to the Malecon.

Malecon is a Spanish word. It means, "place where the natives make a killing renting their boats to tourists who don't know their portholes from their poop decks."

I arrive at the Malecon at 6:30, which is an hour and half before the first boats are scheduled to cast off with their parties of amateur fishermen. But I have to be here early, because once again my travel agency ("No Comprende Holidays Inc.") has failed to make the right connections for me.

After an hour of prowling the waterfront, I finally find four men who agree to let me join them on the boat they have chartered. Shortly after 8 a.m. we are gliding through Acapulco Bay, heading for the Pacific Ocean.

There are eight of us on the boat. The captain, Victor, and his crew, Pedro and Bernardo, are Mexicans. My fishing companions, Tom, Bill, Alex and Tom are Macedonians. From Toronto. As we chug toward the briny deep, it is unclear to me whether we are a fishing party or a United Nations convention.

The name of our boat is the Marlin. It is a 35-footer that has seen better days. But not recently. I'm no expert on boats, but I'm pretty sure that the newer ones aren't designed so that the exhaust billows into the cabin.

Ten miles out, Victor indicates that it is time to begin fishing. Since there are only four fishing chairs on the Marlin, we will have to take turns fishing. We decide that, for the first shift, we will just keep the positions we have had for the past hour.

Tom and Alex will continue to sit in the chairs on the upper deck. Bill and the other Tom will continue to sit in the chairs on the lower deck. I will continue to lean over the side.

After half an hour without any bites, Alex offers to switch. He gives me his seat on the upper deck. I give him my spot on the railing.

It is 9:35 when I settle into the seat for my first attempt at deep sea fishing. Standing at my side, Pedro baits my hook, sets my reel, tosses my line into the water and goes to sit down.

At 9:50 he jumps up and races to my side.

"You have a strike, senor."

"Huh?" I say, flashing the icy-cool presence of mind that has brought me fame on each of the seven seas.

"It's a fish, a fish," he yells.

"Ohmygosh," I say, fumbling for the reel in a display of the cat-quick reflexes that have made my name a legend on the bounding main.

"I've got it," Pedro shouts, seizing control of the rod and reel. He pushes some buttons, flips some levers, does something with the line.

"Now," he says, "reel it in."

The battle begins.

It is just me and the fish. The fish and I. The primeval saga of man against nature. The fish is fighting for his very survival, and he is in his element. I have nothing on my side but my wits, a couple hundred bucks worth of gear, three Mexicans, four Macedonians from Toronto and a 35-foot boat with twin engines.

After a 10-minute struggle, I am tired but triumphant. The

fish is at the side of the boat and Bernardo is leaning over to gaff it.

"What is it?" I call down to him.

"Bonito," he says. "Tuna." I climb down to the lower deck and join Bernardo as he pulls the fish out of the water and smacks it several times on the head with a stick. This does not kill the fish. But it gives it a terrible headache.

It is a beautiful fish, two feet long and silver blue in color. For $40 a foot I can have it stuffed, mounted and shipped home to hang on my wall.

But I decide not to do that. After all, what have I done that is worth bragging about? Pedro did all the preparation and reeled it in. Bernardo hauled the fish over the side. All I did was turn the handle on the reel. Heck, a gorilla could have done that.

Then again, where are you gonna find a gorilla dumb enough to get up at 6 in the morning?

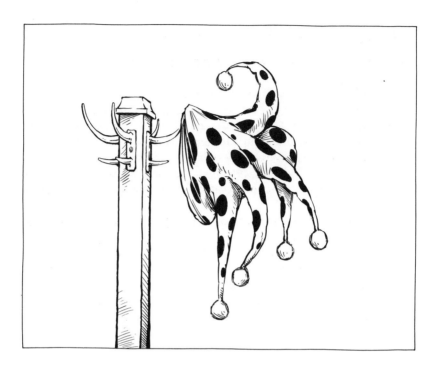

7 The Clown's Day Off

I hate it when opera stars sing Barry Manilow or when stand-up comics read Shakespeare. But sometimes opera stars tire of Verdi and sometimes stand-up comics get sick of telling Billy Carter jokes.

And sometimes humor columnists take life seriously.

That doesn't happen often. But when it does, you seize the moment with both hands and drag it to the nearest typewriter and hope that the readers will understand.

Hello, I'm Your Little Brother

Mar. 6, 1976

KANSAS CITY, Mo. — Sitting alone in this restaurant near the airport, there is plenty of time to reflect on just how little I know about the man I am supposed to meet here.

His name is David Jermann and he is a few years older than I am, I know that. And he lives somewhere near Shawnee Mission, Kan., with a wife and kids and a job doing something or other for TWA.

That's not very much, really. Not very much at all to know about your only brother.

There is no need to go into the reasons why my brother and I are strangers. We are, that's all. We grew up in different homes and the one time we did meet was long ago and only for a few seconds.

Now that we are grown there is no real reason for us to get together just because of our biological coincidence. But there is no reason not to, either.

So I called him a few weeks ago. Called the number that I got from the Kansas City operator to tell him that I would be stopping near his town. Called to see if maybe he might want to meet and have a drink or something.

And that was awkward, because when he answered the phone I had to introduce myself. "David? My name is Denny Stewart . . . I'm your brother."

There was a pause after that and for a moment I was afraid he was going to say, "So what?" But he didn't. He just said yeah, he'd be interested in getting together.

So we set up this meeting at the restaurant near the airport and now he is 15 minutes late and it suddenly occurs to me that I don't even know what he looks like and he doesn't know what I look like, either. What if he walks in here and we don't recognize each other and he just turns around and goes home?

Probably he looks like me, I reason. So I study each man who walks into the restaurant, looking for one with a pot gut and hair that needs cutting.

Then a man is walking toward my table. A man who looks something like me, only better, with no pot gut showing beneath his expensive looking suit. And hair that doesn't need cutting.

How many times in the last few weeks have I tried to imagine this moment, trying to picture how it would be, what we would say. A thousand? Ten thousand? But now that the moment is here, all that happens is that I stand up and we shake hands.

"Hello," he says. "It's nice to see you."

"Hi. Have a chair."

It is hard for me to remember what was said after that. But it was easy talking with him, I remember that. Easier than I had expected.

He is a copilot with TWA, I learn, which helps explain why there is no pot gut showing beneath the expensive looking suit. Pilots are expected to stay in shape, he points out, and they have to take frequent physicals. I point out that newspaper columnists never have to take tests, physical or mental.

We learn a lot of things about each other in the next few hours. We both like sports, we discover. And Jaguars and Miller's beer and after we have a few Miller's we both have to excuse ourselves from the table frequently.

We learn, too, that there are some things we don't have in common. He is left-handed and fast of foot and possessed of the ability to grow sideburns.

We talk about these things and other things, like how I might have grown up differently if I had had a big brother to push me around and how he might have grown up differently if he had had a little brother to pester him. And we laugh a lot and we drink a lot of Miller's and we excuse ourselves from the table frequently.

And soon, too soon, a waitress comes around and says that it is closing time.

We could go up to my hotel room and talk some more, but he has a long drive home and I have a train to catch in the morning. So we empty our glasses and we walk out into the cold night air to where his car is parked and we shake hands for the second time in our lives.

Maybe we'll get together again sometime, we tell each other. Sure, I fly into Dayton a lot. Yeah, and maybe I'll make it back to KC for the convention this summer. Sure, we'll get together again. Sure.

"Well, drive carefully," I say.

"Don't worry," he says. "And listen, lose a little weight and get a haircut, will ya?"

And then he is in his car, driving away. And I am glad about that. I don't think I could stand it if my big brother saw me with tears in my eyes.

Kim and Clifford and, Most of All, Tony

Apr. 30, 1977

Editor's Note: Off the Beat columnist D.L. Stewart attended the local Special Olympics games for retarded people in Montgomery, Greene, Preble and Miami counties in 1976 and wrote this column. It was selected by the Joseph P. Kennedy Jr. Foundation for a Special Olympics Award for distinguished service to the mentally retarded through sports, and won first place in the Ohio Associated Press feature story category.

This is for Kim, who showed me courage, and it is for Clifford, who showed me joy.

But mostly, this is for Tony, who helped me grow.

We met Saturday at the Special Olympics, Tony and I, on an afternoon when dingy clouds scudded over Welcome Stadium and threatened to wash away a lot of work by a lot of volunteers.

And if that had happened, I guess I wouldn't have been too unhappy, because the Special Olympics are mainly for mentally retarded kids, and I have never been very comfortable around persons with mental handicaps. Some of them talk funny and some of them look strange and I have always shied away from them as if what they had would somehow rub off on me.

So for a long time, I stood on the fringe while they ran their races, these kids with IQs of 80 or less, hoping that it wouldn't rain and ruin all the effort that had gone into this, but hoping that it would so that I could go home where no eyes stared vacantly and no jaws hung slackly.

Then a woman asked me if I'd like to be a hugger. A hugger, she explained, was a volunteer who stood at the finish line and made sure that every competitor was rewarded with an encouraging word and maybe a pat on the back when he completed a race.

I didn't want to do it, not really, even though it sounded like a beautiful idea. But I couldn't tell the woman that, so I walked over to the finish line where some other huggers were standing and when a race was completed I tried to pick out kids who appeared the most normal to pat on the back.

After a few races I wandered away, moving to the other side of the field, far from the woman who was recruiting huggers.

That's when I first saw Tony.

He was in a small group of kids in wheelchairs, victims, someone explained, of cerebral palsy, which afflicts the body as well as the mind. Like the others, Tony had gnarled hands and twisted legs and a tongue that didn't always do what he wanted it to when he tried to speak.

But Tony was older than the other kids. He was 21, I learned, and a graduate of Roosevelt High School.

And I stopped to watch Tony's event, which was the softball throw.

I watched Ruby, who is 8, throw the ball with all her strength and saw her smile triumphantly when it landed five feet ahead. I watched Chris, who is 14, hold the ball for several painful minutes without understanding that he was supposed to throw it.

I watched while a volunteer tried to hand the ball to Kim, who is 12, only to have it fall from her lifeless fingers. Again and again, the ball was retrieved. Again and again, she struggled to grip it and I could only wonder how many times I would have tried.

Then it was Tony's turn and I watched him flip the ball a full 10 feet. I started to walk away then, but I was intercepted by a kid who said that somebody wanted to talk to me. And he pointed to Tony, who was nodding and grinning in my direction.

Reluctantly, I walked over to him, waiting uncomfortably while he struggled to form his words.

Who was I, he wanted to know, so I told him, not really sure if he understood what a newspaper writer is.

There was a long silence after that and, because I couldn't think of anything else to say, I asked him if he liked baseball.

Tony grinned and nodded and said, "Reds."

He had difficulty speaking and I had difficulty understanding the half-toned words, but somehow we talked and he told me he didn't think the Reds would win the Series again. Bad pitching, he said. And he showed me his Roosevelt class ring and his leather wrist strap that said "Tony."

And then we were playing catch, Tony and I, his throws coming in hard and true from a distance of six feet and each time I would yell in mock complaint, "Hey, Tony, what are you trying to do, put a hole in me?" He would grin a little more and throw a little harder.

Later, Tony said, "I hungry," so I pushed him to the concession stand and we got a hot dog and a Mountain Dew and then we went back to the track to watch some races.

The best race was the one in which Clifford came in fourth and the judges gave him a green ribbon which somebody pinned to his T-shirt, and he walked around showing his ribbon to everyone and wearing a smile of exquisite joy. It made no difference to Clifford that he had finished fourth in a four-man race. He knew only the child's sense of happiness at having been rewarded for a good effort. Clifford is 47.

Finally, the man who was responsible for helping Tony get home came along, so I said goodby to them. As I walked away, I heard Tony's voice calling out to me and I turned around.

"What did you say, Tony?"

"Ah-ah-ank you."

No, Tony.

Thank you.

. . . for the World is Mine

May 3, 1977

I sighed because the day was dark—and then I met a child who had no eyes.

More than 500 mentally or physically handicapped persons came to Welcome Stadium Saturday to run and throw and jump in the Special Olympics.

They competed in wheelchairs, or with limbs that bent in all the wrong places, or with minds that did not always comprehend.

Most of them were kids, their bodies far too small for the heavy burdens placed on them by cerebral palsy and spinal meningitis, accidents and birth defects.

For two hours, I watched as these kids faced the challenge of running 25 yards without stopping. I listened to their sounds of joy after they had struggled to throw a softball 15 feet.

It was not until later, when I was home again, that I realized what I had not seen or heard. I had seen no tears. I heard no sighs.

I complained because the walk was long—until I met a man who had no legs.

Amy has dark eyes and white ribbons in her long brown hair and everything a little girl of eight should have. Except that, below her ribs, she has no spine.

They call it sacrum hygenesis.

"When she was born, the doctors said she would never get out of bed," says her father.

But with the help of nine operations and crutches and a brace that makes a lump inside the back of her T-shirt, Amy is standing next to me at the south end of the stadium. There is a blue ribbon pinned to her T-shirt.

"I won first place in the softball throw," she says.

"That's very good."

"Yeah. I beat the boys."

Then Amy runs off to enter the 25-yard dash and I ask her father what the big problems are in raising a handicapped child.

He has difficulty finding an answer.

"I guess," he says finally, "the fact that she has no control over her bladder is a little bit of a problem. She has to wear Pampers all the time."

The only problem Amy's mother can think of is finding clothes for her. When they measured Amy last week, she was 36 inches tall.

Amy's brother, 10-year-old Mark, has had the most difficult adjustment.

Sometimes, according to Amy, "he fights with me."

But other times, their father says: "I'll go past his room at night and he'll be crying, just bawling, because he doesn't want her to be crippled."

In spite of that, Mark and Amy's parents see no reason to feel sorry for themselves.

"You can always find somebody with worse problems," their father says.

I prayed for wealth beyond my need—and then I met a poor soul with no bread at all.

Linda's daughter did not compete in the local Special Olympics this year. Linda's daughter is in a residential training center in Springfield. It is unlikely that she will ever be able to come home again.

"There was damage to her spine when she was born," Linda says. "She is profoundly retarded as well as physically handicapped."

Linda was able to take care of her daughter until she was 13. But now she is 16 and literally too big for Linda to handle.

The most difficult thing about raising a multi-handicapped child, Linda says, was the strain it put on the rest of the family.

"You're living two different lives if you have other children in the family," she says. "I have an older son and it would embarrass him when his friends would be at our house and she would wet her pants.

"We almost lost him a couple of times. When he was 4 or 5, and then again when he was a young teen-ager, he withdrew. He would just stay in his room all day."

Linda's son is 20 now and he is studying medicine—which she sees as a positive result of her daughter's handicaps. But it does not always work out that way. Some families do grow together from the experience of having a retarded or handicapped child but others break.

"It can be tough," Linda admits. "Damn tough."

She points to the track, where several kids are struggling to reach the finish line.

"You're seeing the best of it here."

Oh, God, forgive me—for the world is mine.

An Everyday, Blind Belly Dancer

Jan. 24, 1976

It was shortly after she had lost her sight and she was walking somewhat uncertainly down the hospital corridor.

A young man noticed her and her white cane.

"Oh," the young man exclaimed, "did you hurt your leg?"

"No," she replied, "I'm a shepherd."

★ ★ ★

Her name is Connie Green and she's just your everyday, blind, belly-dancing former student nun.

She lives in an ordinary house in Kettering, with four ordinary kids and an ordinary Doberman who plays blackjack.

Like most other blind, belly-dancing former student nuns, 38-year-old Connie Green occupies herself with mundane activities: Roller skating, learning Arabic, sliding down Suicide Hill in Hills and Dales Park and displaying her belly dancing abilities at such places as Courthouse Square.

Connie Green's life wasn't always so routine.

As a youngster in Brooklyn she lived at a Catholic girls' boarding school.

"The nuns were kissing the ground when I left," she recalls. "But it didn't do them any good, because I went back when I was 17 to become a nun myself."

It is a tribute to the endurance of the Roman Catholic Church that it survived her one year as a rookie nun. She was, she relates, into everything. Among the things she was into was a dumbwaiter, which is where she was discovered one evening by the Mother Superior, smuggling contraband sandwiches out of the kitchen.

But it was not until she conspired to include a roulette wheel among the equipment for a religious retreat that the good sisters decided not to press the church's luck any further. Novice Connie was advised to get out of the habit. Or, as she tells her kids now, she flunked out as a nun.

In 1957, she married an aeronautical engineer, a union that was worth 17 years and four offspring before ending in divorce. Five and a half years ago she lost 95 percent of her sight to an affliction the doctors call macular degeneration.

Connie Green, run-of-the-mill blind belly dancer; David Thompson, who's looking for the music in everything; Tempest Storm, a legend you can still see a lot of; and the Administration Building at Ellis Island, the crumbling gateway to America.

The remaining 5 percent enables her to distinguish light from dark and to make out vague shapes. Sometimes she can even read her favorite morning newspaper, if she holds it right up against her face.

"I am the only woman in Dayton with paper cuts on her nose," she says.

Having difficulty in reading *The Journal Herald* is, naturally, the most distressing aspect of what Connie Green calls her "inconvenience." But there are other problems.

"Cooking at the beginning was hilarious," she says. "Everything I served was an ash.

"And a couple of times I sprayed my hair with deodorant and brushed my teeth with hair cream when somebody forgot to put things back where they belonged."

Although Connie Green frequently jokes about her inconvenience (when someone stumbles, she invariably offers them the use of her guide dog), there are some very real problems. Not being able to drive is one. The extra time involved in cleaning house is another.

"What I miss the most is not being able to see peoples' faces, not being able to catch their expressions," she says. "But there's a good side to that, too. Now I see the real personality because I don't just look at the physical person."

Connie Green obviously has adjusted to her inconvenience, which is more than can be said for a lot of folks who came into contact with her.

"Some people are determined to help you across the street, whether you want to go or not," she points out. "And when you go into a restaurant, they do one of two things. Either they hand you a menu, which doesn't do me much good, or they ask the person with you things like, 'Does she want cream in her coffee?' like I can't even answer for myself.

"What really gets me, though, is the people who think they have to yell to make you hear them. You sit there saying to yourself, 'What am I, blind AND deaf?' "

Because she never became very adroit at handling a cane ("I was forever getting it stuck in the sidewalk gratings and poking people"), Connie Green travels with the help of a guide dog.

But not even the dog is safe from her barbs. When it bumps into things, Connie Green threatens to buy it a seeing-eye cat.

The guide dog, whose name is Suzie, is not to be confused with the Doberman, whose name is Biz. Biz earns his keep as a watchdog and card shark.

"He can smile and play 21," Connie Green insists. "The damndest thing about it is, he wins." Which is not really all that remarkable, when you stop and think about it. I mean, who's gonna tell a Doberman that he lost?

But Connie Green seldom has time these days to sit around dealing cards to Biz. She is usually too busy in a whirl of volunteer work and socializing and having water fights out on the lawn with her four kids.

Just like any other blind belly-dancing former student nun.

'There Is Music in Everything'

Aug. 30, 1975

This is David Thompson's story.

It is not a particularly important story, I guess, when you compare it to all the really significant ones today. It's just about a young man with long hair who plays a flute and sometimes sits around listening to a waterfall and hearing music other people don't hear. If you have something important to do, please go ahead and turn the page.

David Thompson visited our office awhile back for a reason that is no more important than this story. He carried his flute under his arm and his long, light hair brushed his shoulders with each step and a couple of people glanced up and said, "Is that a boy or a girl?" and then went back to what they were doing.

David Thompson, who is tall and thin and 22 years old, is used to such comments, but long hair is a part of him, just as music is a part of him.

The music came first, starting when he was seven years old and a ward of the Ohio Soldiers and Sailors Orphans Home in Xenia. David Thompson hated the home and only his music lessons with George Schumacher made it bearable there. But after awhile not even the music was enough and he was kicked out of the orphanage when he was 14. Then he went to Stebbins High School, where his most lasting impression came from five guys who beat him up "because my sister married a black man."

It was sometime after that that David Thompson deserted the clarinet and saxophone in favor of a flute.

"A flute is just more sensitive," he says, "you can be more creative with it. With a flute, you're the one that's limited, not the horn."

David Thompson spends a great deal of his time trying to stretch the limits of himself to match the potential of his instrument. Last year he went to Yellow Springs and fasted for four days to cleanse himself and become more sensitive. He spent the daytimes in the woods, listening to the sound of a waterfall, hearing the rapid buildup of water, the cascade of it falling, the crash of it hitting the stream that had preceded it.

From his pilgrimage to the waterfall has come the "Waterfall Suite," which he hopes to record on an album along with "Prayer at Dawn," which is the sound of frost on a leaf.

For awhile, David Thompson tried to stretch the limits of himself artificially, with the crutch of drugs.

"I started messing with drugs in 1968," he says without apology. "But drugs, that's not even a part of me anymore. I haven't done that for three and a half years."

It has not always been easy, not doing drugs anymore. He says he was picked up while hitchhiking recently "by two hippie cats and they wanted me to smoke pot with them. When I wouldn't do it, they beat the crap out of me. One of them said, 'What's the matter, man, you straight or something?'

"I don't dig long-haired people too much anymore," David Thompson adds, shaking his head and seemingly unaware of the long hair that falls over his face.

Many things make David Thompson sad. Rock music, with "all those clowns dressed in costumes playing electric garbage" makes him sad. The Victoria Opera House makes him sad for not living up to its potential. Mostly he is saddened by musicians who are afraid to play what they feel.

"This town is very dead musically," he says. "People aren't really creative, they're just playing straight standard stuff. When they have to concentrate, oh man, they get scared."

David Thompson talks dispassionately of orphanages and drugs and beatings, but when he speaks of music he becomes animated.

"There is music in everything," he insists.

Is there music here, in this office, where people are working on their very important stories?

"Sure. Just listen."

And we stop and listen to the clatter of typewriters, to the ringing of telephones, to the rise and fall of conversations. To me it is the sound of a newspaper office. To David Thompson it is music.

"One place I love is city traffic. You have no idea what it is to stand on a bridge and hear the five o'clock traffic go by. You can hear horns and tires and the water from the river and the breeze and the birds. There are changes in rhythm, like when a red light stops traffic.

"I worked in a machine shop and it was really scary, it was so loud and everything. But that was music, too, when I stopped to listen. The machines made the rhythm and people talking over the machines made up the melody line. I'd take my flute to work sometimes and during a break I'd play it."

It is a picture that is hard to project, David Thompson with his long hair playing a flute in a machine shop full of grease and steel and hard hats.

"A lot of people were hippie types, they were willing to listen. The other people were into country music, but I didn't worry about them. You can't get stumbled by them."

David Thompson was out of work when I talked to him, but he had a line on a job with a band.

"I teach flute to this girl and her uncle plays on the Merv Griffin network band. He's coming to Dayton this summer and it's kind of arranged where I'm going to play for this guy. There's no guarantee he can get me into the band . . . there's never a guarantee in music. You have to live from one day to the next."

Talking to David Thompson, it is harder to imagine him in Merv Griffin's apple pie band than it is to picture him in a machine shop. David Thompson sees the incongruity, too, but points out, "I have to think finance. That's a start. Miles Davis and John Coltrane, they both started straight."

It has been awhile since I talked to David Thompson. Maybe he got the job with the Merv Griffin band and got his hair cut and bought a car and is on his way to becoming what is known as a success. But, deep inside, there's something that says I hope he doesn't. Deep inside, I envy David Thompson, with his freedom to sit all alone and listen to the sound of a waterfall.

A Legend Who Still Takes It Off

Oct. 7, 1975

They are almost all gone now, the legends of my youth. Marilyn took too many pills and Lanza ate too much pasta and, gosh, how long has it been since Doby crashed into a centerfield fence and whatever happened to Bob and Justine?

But one that remains (or is it two that remain?) is Tempest Storm, who held a press conference at the Dayton Inn yesterday to call attention to the fact that a great deal of her will be on display this week at the Todd Burlesk.

As press conferences go it was nothing special, except for when a Channel 7 guy asked Tempest what her soon-to-be-published autobiography is all about. A question like that should put its author in the journalism hall of fame, right next to the radio interviewer who once asked the leader of a musical group, "Tell us, how many are there in your quintet?"

But if no great wit was displayed at this press conference, there were at least some other things displayed and all in all I'm glad I went, because how many times do you get to see a legend up close?

To the younger set, to the ones who believe that sex was invented by Linda Lovelace, the name Tempest Storm may not mean a lot. But to those of us who stare into the mirror each morning in apprehensive search of gray, it is a magic name, a name that evokes memories of a time when some delights were still forbidden.

Tempest Storm was, and is, a stripper. In her prime she was reportedly paid $5,000 a week to let people watch her undress, and if that seems ridiculous you must remember that this was in an era in which throats were not nearly so deep and not much went on behind green doors.

At a certain point in adolescence, then, seeing Tempest Storm in the flesh became as urgent as seeing Willie Mays in the outfield. Later, it became more urgent.

And so around the age of 16 you would borrow a draft card that proved you were 18 and you would present it along with your money at the cashier's booth at the Roxy or the Mayfair or wherever. For a few seconds you would squirm and try to look older and maybe stoop down a little because you were six-foot tall and the draft card said you were 5-9.

But almost invariably they would be fooled by your deception, because if they kept out everyone who was underage they wouldn't make enough to pay the light bill.

Inside, the stage lights made it bright up front and shadowy in the back, so you sat in the back, where teen-age pimples were in the majority. And even though you couldn't see the stage as well, you were glad to be back there because you just wouldn't have felt as comfortable up front with all the bald heads.

So you sat near the back and watched the second and third stringers perform and listened to the comics say racy things like "what the hey" and "son of a biscuit." And if you were rich enough and dumb enough you bought a box of taffy, because the guy on the stage guaranteed that there was a special prize inside each and every box. And maybe you even bought a special mirror they were selling, because if you held it to the light in a certain way, the guy said, you would see some very, very interesting scenes. It wasn't until you were on your way home that you gave serious thought as to why your box of taffy was the only one that didn't have a special prize in it and how come your mirror only showed you your own reflection.

By the time the first team arrived onstage in high heels and long gloves and sparkly gown you had pretty much had your fill of spectator sex. But you stayed there anyway, because how could you go back to the pizza house and admit to everybody there that you got up and walked out without ever seeing Tempest Storm take it off?

So you watched her take off the long gloves and the sparkly gown and pretty soon all that remained were the high heels, the pasties and a G-string. If you squinted, you could almost convince yourself that no one else was there, just you and Tempest Storm. If you squinted even more, you could almost convince yourself that the pasties and G-string weren't there either.

But no matter how hard you squinted, you could never make any connection between the woman on the stage and any real girls that you might know. Not even with Ginny Martin, who had the fullest sweater in the whole school.

Of course, all of this was long ago and much has happened since then. Marilyn is gone and Lanza is gone and Doby no longer crashes into fences and if Bob and Justine still dance, they don't do it together.

But Tempest Storm, at the age of 47, remains 41-21-38.
And if the 41 droops a little closer to the 21, what of it? How
often do you get to take a second look at a legend of your
youth?

Still a Message at America's Gateway

July 9, 1977

NEW YORK — It is a rainy, windy, thoroughly disagreeable day and on the ferryboat built for 400, I am the only
passenger.

As the boat chugs through the drab water, the Statue of
Liberty half a mile off our port bow, I am aware that some of
the crew are watching me. I can guess what they are thinking:

Why would anybody come out on a day like this just to
visit Ellis Island?

It is a question I am not quite sure how to answer.

It is not, to be certain, the kind of place where I am likely
to find funny things to write about. For many of the 12 million
immigrants who passed through it between 1800 and 1954, Ellis
Island may well have been the Gateway to America.

But for many others, it was the Island of Tears. It was a
place where families were divided and spirits were broken and
dreams died.

My grandfather was one of the 12 million, an immigrant
from Rumania on his way to Cleveland to join his brother as a
baker.

But that's not what draws me, either. Roots hold no appeal
for me. What my grandfather was really doesn't interest me
that much. I am far more concerned with what my children
might become.

As the "Miss Freedom" glides into its docking position at
Ellis Island, I still have not been able to answer my own
question. I still am not sure why I have come here on this grey,
forbidding day.

Then there is no time for further introspection because the
gangplank is down and I am sprinting through the rain, dodging
puddles on the walk that leads to the main building.

A guide is waiting for me at the door. Her name is Elaine

and she wears the uniform of the National Park Service, which opened the island for public tours last year.

Elaine is young and rather pretty. Also, she is black. There is, it seems to me, a certain irony in that. Her ancestors probably did not come through Ellis Island.

"Ellis Island was originally three separate islands," she begins in brisk, tour-guide fashion. "As a result of landfilling, it is now two islands. In 1897, fire . . ."

For a moment, I tune Elaine out. I don't care much about fires that happened in 1897. I would much rather just stand here for awhile and close my eyes and feel this place. To experience it. Not as it is now, with broken tiles and crumbling bricks and walls shored up with 2 by 4s.

But to experience it as it was then, when my grandfather walked through these rooms, filled with hope and worry and emotions that I can only guess about.

What has gone wrong?

I would be here only a few hours, they told me, to answer some questions, to be examined by the doctors. Then I would be given a landing pass and sent on my way.

But I have been here for three days and still there is no word. They are trying to contact my brother, they say. Be patient. Be patient.

If I had more money, I would not have to be patient. The rich ones on our boat, the passengers in first and second class, they did not have to be patient.

For them, small boats came alongside and doctors came aboard.

But there were no small boats for those of us in steerage. For us, there was a barge to bring us to this huge, Romanesque building filled with so many rooms.

In the first room, the baggage room, we are told to leave our belongings. They will be safe here, the interpreter says. Otherwise, the runners might get us.

Runners, they explain, are men who wait at the Battery for the people who are carrying luggage when they get off the boat. Then they grab the suitcase and run away with it.

"A runner is a thief, then?" I ask the interpreter.

"No, no," he says. "He does not mean to keep the suitcase. He only wants you to chase him to the hotel that has employed him for this purpose. There you will be persuaded to stay for the night."

"If a runner tries to take my suitcase, I will fight him," says a large man from Warsaw.

"While you are fighting him, another runner may take your child," the interpreter answers.

I am glad I have no children. On the ship, so many got sick. But it is not surprising. I, myself, did not feel well. The water was rough and there was little room and the food was poor. Fish and potato soup nearly every day.

A young man from Zurich said a very funny thing about the food. On the fourth day they served us potato soup, he said:

"When I get to America, I will never look another potato in the eye."

After we are finished in the baggage room, we are led to a huge room with high arched ceilings and row after row of wooden benches.

"This is the registry room," the interpreter tells us. "Listen for the numbers. When the number that is called matches the number that is pinned to your coat, report to the infirmary."

For an hour I sit on a wooden bench in the registry room, listening to the numbers being called and the babies crying and the conversations all around me. Some of the languages I recognize. My own, of course. And German. Italian. A little bit of Greek.

But there are so many that sound only like so much gibberish. Like English. It is such a strange language. Learning the others was not hard, but I doubt if I will ever be able to speak English.

Eventually my number is called and I climb the iron stairway that leads to the infirmary. The stairs are steep and the man in front of me, an older man from the Ukraine, is breathing heavily by the time he reaches the top.

There he is stopped by a doctor and a letter "H" is pinned to his coat. I learn later that it is because the doctor suspects that the man may have heart trouble. The doctors in the infirmary will examine him closely.

It is surprising that the old man was allowed to board the ship in the first place. When immigrants are refused admission, the steamship company must pay for their return fare.

I pass my physical examination easily. I am young and strong.

Then I return to the registry room. All that remains now is to answer some questions. Most of the questions, I have been told, are intended to trip up those who will not be able to find honest work.

Some countries, when times are bad, release inmates from prisons and mental asylums and send them here, hoping to be rid of their expense. And women have been brought here for immoral purposes. That is why single women are not allowed to leave the island without a male escort — a father, husband, fiance.

To make sure that the men who present themselves as fiances are not merely procurers, marriages are performed here on the island.

Devious people, Americans.

Finally, my number is called a second time. I jump up and a guard directs me to a stern-looking official sitting behind a table.

"What is your name?" he says. "Your trade? What country are you from? How much money do you have? Let me see it."

The questions come rapidly, but I manage to answer them all. Not like the man from Turkey, who became so confused during the questioning that he gave the name of his town when they asked what his own name was. Now all of his papers list his name as "Constantinople."

And I spoke last night to two brothers from Italy who were summoned at the same time, but to different officials' tables. "Virende," their name was. But, at one table, an extra "e" was added to the name. And, at the other table, the original "e" was removed.

After I have finished answering my questions, I am told to return to my seat and wait to be called again. There is a problem.

Shaking, I return to my seat, unable to understand what kind of a problem there could be. In his last letter, my brother said that this would be easy, that as many as 5,000 immigrants a day come through here and only two percent are returned.

The only thing I really had to worry about, he said, was not to be cheated when I bought my train ticket to Cleveland. Some clerks, he said, would sell tickets from New York to Cleveland by way of Atlanta. This, he explained, was like going from Bucharest to Zagreb by way of Khaskovo.

But now, perhaps, I will not need a train ticket. It has been three days, and still I have not been called to appear before the special board of inquiry that will decide my case.

Three days of waiting. Three days of sleeping in the dormitory with dozens of men who even snore in strange languages. Three days of eating the usual foods that are served in the dining hall.

Last night at supper, a woman from Ireland became hysterical when the servers put spaghetti and tomato sauce on her plate. She thought they were going to force her to eat worms.

I, myself, had problems with a fruit, the inside of which was soft and sweet, but the outside of which was very tough and difficult to swallow. I do not understand why people eat bananas.

It is all very confusing, this island.

In the dormitory at night, long after the lights are out, I lie there and I think about runners and the special board of inquiry and bananas and cities with unpronounceable names like Philadelphia and Minneapolis.

And I think about home and wonder if perhaps I have made a mistake. It is very lonely on this island. And sometimes, I am frightened.

★ ★ ★

The tour has lasted just under an hour-and-a-half. As Elaine leads me back to the main entrance, I can see through the window that the rain has slowed.

I thank her and I walk back to the waiting boat, the boat that will take me to the Battery, just the way a boat must have taken my grandfather.

As we chug through the drab water, the Statue of Liberty

now on the starboard side, I look back at Ellis Island. The
Gateway to America. The Island of Tears.

I know now what I was looking for when I boarded "Miss
Freedom" on this rainy, windy, thoroughly disagreeable day.

I was looking for courage.

They Just Want to Make Friends

Sept. 3, 1976

I don't care what anybody says, I think this whole
desegregation thing was a big waste of time.

I mean, here all us adults are doing this planning and wor-
rying and speech-making and proclamation-issuing and edito-
rial-writing and all-night-prayer-vigiling . . . and what good has
it done?

Those kids don't even appreciate it.

Like, I went out to Franklin School on East Fifth Street
yesterday, just to see how the kids there were bearing up under
all this pressure. I'll bet I talked to two dozen kids and not a one
of them said anything about EQUAL EDUCATION or HAR-
MONIOUS RACIAL CO-EXISTENCE.

I hate to say this but I'll bet some of those kids didn't even
read the proclamations.

For instance, I talked to this girl Theresa, who is 11 years
old. Theresa is white and she has always gone to Franklin,
which was the only all-white school in the Dayton system last
year.

"What do you think about school this year?" I ask her, and
I sort of let my eyes drift around the lunchroom, but I don't say
the word "desegregation" because you're supposed to pretend
like nothing has changed.

"It's all right now," Theresa says. "But later on it's going
to be hard."

Hard?

"Yeah. 'Cause pretty quick we have to start on social
studies. I hate social studies."

There are a whole lot more questions I want to ask
Theresa, but I never get a chance because right away she starts
giggling and whispering into the ear of the black girl who is sitting next to her.

So I just walk away, shaking my head and wondering how Theresa is ever going to develop a SOCIAL CONSCIOUSNESS if she keeps on that way.

Then I talk to a bunch of fifth-grade boys at the next table. They are Kenneth and Norman and Tyrone and Kevin, who were bused here from Edison School, which was 99.3 percent black last year. Sitting in their midst is Mike, who is white.

First off, it's difficult to get them to answer me, seeing as they are all so busy laughing and joking and punching each other in the arms.

But finally I get Kenneth's attention and I ask him about CROSS-DISTRICT BUSING.

"It's neat," Kenneth says. "Everytime the bus hits a bump we all go whoooeee." And he lifts up off his chair to show what happens when the bus hits a bump.

What about you, Tyrone? What do you think about being here in this school instead of Edison?

"I like it," Tyrone says. And before I can ask him if he likes it because he feels CROSS-TOWN PUPIL ASSIGNMENT will appreciably enhance his prospects for SOCIO-ECONOMIC AD-VANCEMENT, Tyrone explains:

"At Edison we had to work hard on the first day. That's why I like it better here. You get to play more."

And Kenenth and Norman and Mike and Tyrone and Kevin all resume their laughing and joking and punching each other in the arms. It is obvious that they do not understand that they are part of a LANDMARK DECISION.

So I try again with Randy, who has bright, red hair and Darryl, who has a small, trim Afro. But they are busy talking about football and airplanes.

And Tammy and Yvette are giggling and the black kid at the next table is having a pretend boxing match with the white kid next to him and a white kid is telling a black kid that it must be neat to be black because if you get a black eye it won't show and finally I give it all up and head back to the office.

It has been a truly discouraging morning. *The New York Times* is in town and all three TV networks are here and the eyes of the state, if not the nation, are focused on Dayton, Ohio, for this SOCIALLY SIGNIFICANT day.

But a lot these kids care. All they want to do is sit around making friends.

Why Don't They Let 'Rags' Be Happy?

July 19, 1977

I see where they're trying to deface another Dayton landmark.

According to a story the other day in a local paper which is always a step behind *The Journal Herald*, some merchants want police to clean up the man they call "Rags."

The merchants say he looks bad. And he smells bad. And sometimes he goes to the bathroom where he shouldn't.

If you have spent any time at all in downtown Dayton, you have seen the man they call "Rags." He is as much a part of the downtown scene as parking meters and the girls of Sixth and Ludlow.

He wears rags on his back and rags on his feet and he wanders downtown without apparent purpose, sometimes walking, sometimes standing and watching life hurry by.

In a big city like New York or L.A., where there are lots of "Rags," he wouldn't be noticed much. But in Dayton, Ohio, he is a curiosity and people tend to point and stare when he is around.

There are a lot of theories about "Rags."

He comes from Connecticut. He comes from Wisconsin. He comes from the South.

He is a Commie. He is a defrocked minister. He is a CIA agent.

His real name is Elisa John Baraunskas. His real name is Howard Hughes.

But no one knows for sure, because "Rags" keeps to himself mostly, avoiding reporters the same way he avoids offers of new clothes.

Which was fine with me, because in my fantasies "Rags" was always a rich man who had his butler lay out his tattered shreds each morning and then traveled downtown to lounge around and inwardly laugh at us as we raced from here to there in search of bigger and better ulcers.

So I never attempted to interview him, because I feared the truth would not be nearly as much fun.

I was surprised when he approached me one day last spring and asked if I could spare some change. I had never seen him with his hand out. I had never even heard of it. I had only heard about all the times he had refused offers of clothing, even when it was 20-below.

I dug around in my pocket and came up with a quarter. Then, because he seemed to be heading in my direction, I walked along Fourth Street with him, asking him questions.

His name, he said, is Lee. He is from "all over" and he spent last winter "here and there" and he has been in Dayton "for awhile."

At Ludlow Street he went one way and I went the other.

Although the ingredients were meager, I thought about doing a column on that meeting. A lot of people had suggested that I write about him some day.

I'm not sure why I didn't. I guess because "Rags" had made it pretty obvious that he didn't want to be written about and the readers' "right to know" didn't seem to justify an invasion of his privacy.

But now they want "Rags" to be cleaned up and dressed up and made to look respectable.

"About 15 people have contacted me," says Officer Thomas Sammons of the Central Business District police task force. "Mostly merchants. I guess he is offensive to look at and he does smell pretty bad. If you get up close to him, you can see the sores on his body.

"I personally feel he should have some sort of help."

Maybe Officer Sammons is right.

Maybe "Rags" should be cleaned up and dressed up and made to look respectable. Even though he obviously doesn't want that, it would be for his own good. Just as seat belts and motorcycle helmets and warnings on cigarette packs are for our own good.

And maybe the merchants are right, too.

Maybe "Rags" is bad for business, although he has never

been known to bother anybody. And maybe he does smell bad, although smelling bad can't be a crime, or a lot of people I know would be convicts.

So clean him up. Dress him up. Make him look respectable. What right does he have, anyway, to wander in our town . . . minding his own business and being happy?

Santa's Kid Stuff Still Works

Dec. 16, 1975

Michael is 8 years old and he doesn't believe in Santa Claus anymore.

He hasn't believed since last year, when a girl in his class who was too wise for her years spilled the beans and we were forced to admit to him that Santa is just another story that adults have made up for reasons that are not easily explained.

So we didn't give much thought to Michael when he contacted the Kettering Jaycees last week and asked them if they would send one of their Santas to our house for a visit.

This is the third year that the Jaycees have been providing Santas for Kettering area homes. For $5, or $15 for groups, they will send you a Santa for a 15-minute visit. He comes complete with a bag of candy canes and a driver to protect him. Which makes sense, I suppose. Still, it is somewhat depressing to think that Santa Claus needs protection.

In addition to bringing their ho-ho-hos to private homes, the Kettering Santas are available for appearances at churches, Cub Scout groups, adult dance classes and just about anything this side of a topless go-go joint. Not all of Santa's visits are total successes. One Santa fell off a back porch as he was leaving the scene. Another was certain he was captivating his little host when suddenly the kid turned and walked out of the room.

"Where are you going?" his parents called. "I'll be back," the kid said. "But right now it's time for *Adam-12*."

Being careful not to invite any *Adam-12* fans, we have asked some of the neighborhood kids over for our surprise visit by Santa: Karyn and Janie from next door and J.B. from across the street. Along with Eric, who lives in our house, they are known as the Wild Bunch and constitute the main reason that the Mafia is afraid to move into Beavercreek.

Santa is due to arrive at 7:30, so we have told the Wild Bunch to show up at 7:20. We figure that will give them enough time to take off their coats and get settled, but not enough time to dismantle the fireplace and tear off the wallpaper.

By 7:30 they have reduced the Christmas cookies to crumbs and have drunk, spilled or otherwise disposed of the punch. They are starting to cast menacing glances at the fireplace.

Just in time, the sound of bells is heard through the back patio door, followed a moment later by the sight of a large man with white whiskers and a red suit.

For a few seconds the whole herd is speechless, which in itself makes the $15 investment worthwhile.

It is Michael, the non-believer, who first regains control of his tongue.

"WOW," he says.

Then they all return to normal.

Santa has one foot in the door when Janie, who is 3, shouts: "I want a Walking Baby Loves You."

"Why didn't you come down the chimney," demands Karyn, who is 5 and beginning to grow suspicious about the whole routine.

Fortunately, Santa is quick-witted. He points out that there is a rather warm fire going in the fireplace at this particular moment.

"Where's your reindeer?" she persists. "How did you get here?"

Santa, who bears a remarkable resemblance to an NCR employe named John Tschirhart, is a veteran at coping with cross-examination. He handles all the questions deftly and eventually the conversation turns to the list of demands.

"I want a Steve Austin." "I want a drum." "I want a drum, too." "My baby doesn't have any teeth." "I want a J.B." "My mommy's fat, just like you."

Through it all, Michael sits on the couch with his big sister, silent, taking it all in. The discussion now has turned to reindeer. "My favorite is Rudolph." "My favorite is Donder and Blitzer."

Slowly, hesitantly, Michael approaches the man in the red suit whose eyes sort of twinkle through his glasses and whose laugh is so warm. There is no Santa Claus, he knows. It's only your parents. And yet . . .

"Santa," he says quietly, more quietly than I think I have ever heard him before, "my favorite reindeer is Cupid."

And for a moment, a magic moment, toys are made at the North Pole and not in Japan and they come in a sleigh drawn by eight tiny reindeer instead of a Rike's truck and Santa Claus is real and all things are possible for Michael.

Thank you for that moment, Kettering Jaycees. Thank you, Santa.